MARKETING IN A SLOW-GROWTH ECONOMY

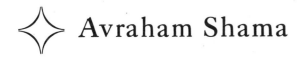 Avraham Shama

MARKETING IN A SLOW-GROWTH ECONOMY

The Impact of Stagflation on Consumer Psychology

PRAEGER

PRAEGER SPECIAL STUDIES • PRAEGER SCIENTIFIC

Library of Congress Cataloging in Publication Data

Shama, Avraham.
    Marketing in a slow-growth economy.

    Bibliography: p.
    Includes index.
    1. Marketing. 2. Inflation (Finance and unemploy-
ment. 3. Consumption (Economics) I. Title.
HF5415.S3964   658.8   79-26312
ISBN 0-03-052151-3

Published in 1980 by Praeger Publishers
CBS Educational and Professional Publishing
A Division of CBS, Inc.
521 Fifth Avenue, New York, New York 10017 U.S.A.

© 1980 by Praeger Publishers

0123456789   038   987654321

Printed in the United States of America

To Louise, Liat, and Dan,

for making life meaningful

PREFACE

This book is about forces that Americans have been confronting since the oil shortage of 1973. It is about the combined impact of inflation, shortages, and recession (defined as stagflation) on lifestyles and consumption patterns. It deals with the obvious and the subtle, the superficial and the significant: the impact of stagflation on consumers; the alarming effects of stagflation on people's hopes, expectations, and values; and the far-reaching implications for the structure and dynamics of business, political life, and American society.

Though the book is written to help business and marketing executives cope with stagflation and be more responsive to the rapidly changing consumer, its study design and discussion of findings go far beyond standard business texts, in that they relate to social processes and their implications as well as to consumer behavior and marketing strategy. This is because of the nature of stagflation and my personal inclination to treat the business-consumption sphere as one dimension of social life.

The net result, I think, is a book that should be of interest not only to those in business and marketing, but also to those interested in consumer psychology, social life, and public opinion.

The book has five chapters. The first discusses modern stagflation and its various forms. Chapters 2-4 are based on my longitudinal study of the impact of stagflation on marketing management and the consumer, and of the resulting social and political implications. The last chapter discusses the post-stagflation society that will emerge, and business strategies.

Stagflation is a long-run phenomenon. The scope and depth of its future impact will depend largely on the way that consumers, business, and government deal with it. In this respect, if the present book is a modest beginning of the study of stagflation and how to cope with it, then the time spent preparing it has been well spent.

ACKNOWLEDGMENTS

I am deeply indebted to Conrad Berenson, chairman of the Marketing Department at Baruch College of the City University of New York, for his comments on various parts of the manuscript, and the encouragement and the supportive environment given me. Also at Baruch College, I would like to thank my colleague Dave Rachman for reading and commenting on early drafts of this manuscript, and Samuel Thomas, the dean of the School of Business, and Provost Philip Austin for supplying some of the resources associated with preparing this book. Special thanks are also extended to Burt Brown of General Mills for making the data of the General Mills 1976 national study of consumers available to me.

Also to be thanked are Maureen Coughlin and Joe Wisenblit—at the time my assistants and later my colleagues at Baruch College—for many hours of hard work involving literature search, manuscript reading, and more. For much of the computer work reported in this manuscript, I would like to thank my assistant Steve Gould, whose abilities in computer communication border on the supernatural. Finally, I owe special gratitude to the students in the Marketing U889 doctoral seminar for many illuminating comments.

Special thanks are also due to Sophie Weintraub for typing the manuscript.

Finally, I would like to thank my wife, Louise, for hours spent discussing inflation with me, and for her comments on the manuscript.

Responsibility for the finished product is, of course, mine alone.

CONTENTS

LIST OF TABLES

LIST OF FIGURES

MARKETING IN A
SLOW-GROWTH
ECONOMY

1
STAGFLATION: AN OVERVIEW

Whether one calls it a "stagnant economy in a time of inflation," "a new inflation," or "any combination of inflation, recession, and shortage," stagflation is an extreme economic force having an impact on most facets of social and political life. In fact, it
is said to define the state not only of the American economy but of
its society and union.

Though not entirely new—it was first discussed by Alvin Hansen
in 1939—stagflation had a limited impact prior to the oil shortage of
1973. The pre-1973 economy was characterized by low rates of inflation (3-4 percent) and unemployment (4-5 percent), and a steady
and meaningful growth of gross national product (GNP) and disposable income from which most segments of the American society
benefited. The post-1973 era, however, represents a stagflation
economy characterized by high rates of inflation (6-13 percent) and
unemployment (6-9 percent), and a slower and less predictable economic growth affecting most Americans.

Furthermore, stagflation is not a uniform concept, nor is
there an agreement as to its causes. Yet, however defined or measured, the scope of stagflation is worldwide, and its impact on business and society is drastic.

The nature, causes, and scope of stagflation are discussed in
this chapter, and the ramifications of stagflation for business and
consumers are outlined. In later chapters particular attention is
given to marketing management and consumers, in order to develop
insights into the problem-solving aspects of marketing.

It also should be noted that although some aspects of stagflation in various countries are pointed out, the main focus in the pre-
sentations and discussions throughout the book relates to stagflation
in the United States. In addition, the reader is advised that the

present book is not a work of economic theory. Rather, it is a book on the marketing and social-psychological impacts of stagflation.

CONTEMPORARY STAGFLATION

Contemporary stagflation began with the oil crisis of 1973. Although it is possible to demonstrate that stagflation is the result of long-term economic and noneconomic processes, only after the oil crisis did the picture of high inflation and high unemployment become unmistakably clear. In the United States, for example, while the inflation rate in 1972 was 3.4 percent, it became 11 percent and 13.1 percent in 1974 and 1975, respectively; similarly, while unemployment was 5.6 percent in 1972, it increased to 8.5 percent and 7.7 percent in 1975 and 1976, respectively (World Bank 1978).

Although most economists agree that stagflation is a mixed economic environment of both low growth and inflation, there is no clear operational definition for the minimal levels of inflation and growth at which stagflation begins. While this point is open to personal opinions and judgments, one can nevertheless presume that stagflation starts at a point where both inflation and unemployment deviate from their traditional, or "normal," or "acceptable" levels. Thus, if the American economy is accustomed to 3-4 percent inflation and 4-6 percent unemployment, then stagflation develops when an increase occurs in these rates. If only one rate increases, one may define the situation as either an inflation or recession.

Nevertheless, stagflation caught economists, marketers, and policy makers by total surprise. "It was not picked up on any of the economic antennae, or foreshadowed in the print-outs of the proliferating computerized econometric models" (Levinson 1971, pp. 13-14). The reason for this is that stagflation is a paradoxical economic environment contradicting both Keynesian notions and the Phillips curve.

According to John Maynard Keynes, problems of inflation can be solved by reducing aggregate demand through the use of contracting fiscal and monetary policies. Using fiscal measures, the government lowers its demand for goods and services, thus reducing the inflationary pressures; using monetary policies, it reduces the availability of money, and hence decreases the amount of money that can chase goods and services and push their prices up. On the other hand, problems of unemployment or recession can be solved by increasing aggregate demand through the use of expansionary fiscal and monetary policies. Using fiscal measures, the government increases its demand for goods and services, thus stimulating the economy to increase employment; and utilizing monetary measures, it increases the amount of money available to the economy, which stimulates consumers to increase their demand for goods and services, and results in increased employment. In other words, according to Keynes there is a trade-off between inflation and unemployment: problems of inflation can be reduced or solved by increasing unemployment, and problems of unemployment may be reduced or solved by increasing aggregate demand and, hence, inflationary pressures (Keynes 1936).

This concept of inflation-unemployment trade-off was empirically tested by A. W. Phillips (1958), whose research findings—though far from conclusive—became the basis for the Phillips curve postulating a trade-off between inflation and unemployment as a general law (depicted in Figure 1.1). As can be seen in Figure 1.1, an increase in the money wage rate, which is always inflationary, in that it pressures prices upward, is associated with a reduction in the unemployment rate. Consequently, "The rate of change of money wage rates can be explained by the level of unemployment and the rate of unemployment" (Phillips 1958, p. 299; for a reappraisal of this concept, see Prudy and Zis 1973).

FIGURE 1.1

Phillips Curve: The Inflation-Unemployment Trade-off

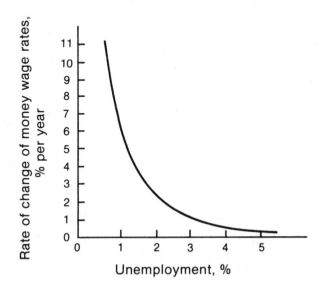

Source: Phillips 1958, p. 297.

In contrast, stagflation is characterized by inflation that does not respond to unemployment, and vice versa. At best, there seems to be little trade-off between inflation and unemployment. That is, the "price" of reducing inflation by one or two percentage points is a very high unemployment rate (Kaldor 1976; Mallen 1977; Prudy and Zis 1973; Reese 1977; Santomero and Seater 1978). Even worse, according to at least one authority, inflation and unemployment seem to reinforce each other within particular ranges (Friedman 1977). Consequently, policies to deal with stagflation, whether fiscal or monetary in nature, cannot be effective because they cannot be designed to expand and contract the economy simultaneously, which is exactly the remedy stagflation calls for (Okun 1975a; 1977).

Though stagflation generally refers to the coexistence of inflation and stagnant growth or recession, it is important to note that different inflation and recession mixes may denote different types of stagflation in terms of scope, depth, and policies or coping strategies. In addition, one may add shortage as another stagflation ingredient. Accordingly, Avraham Shama (1978) argues that stagflation may be defined as any combination of inflation, recession, and shortage.

To most marketers stagflation represents a situation in which demand is stagnant, yet prices must be raised in order to do the following:

Compensate for the higher prices of materials and labor, that is, to compensate for cost-push inflation
Account for higher fixed and overhead costs that result from idle capacity
Account for anticipated inflation
Achieve a certain target profit.

As will be demonstrated in Chapter 2, such a strategy can be counterproductive, in that it may decrease both sales and profits.

CAUSES

Though there is a consensus that stagflation describes a slow-growth or no-growth economy during periods of inflation, opinions vary as to its cause or causes. Understandably, because stagflation is a new and unfamiliar macroeconomic and social phenomenon, all that researchers can do is make attributions and inferences as to the cause(s) of stagflation, and support them by whatever data are available.

It has been suggested that stagflation is caused by lack of competition or by monopolistic market powers; the labor unions; the federal government as a consumer and regulator; international forces; and secular forces such as population change and technological innovations.

Monopoly Power

Monopoly power relates to the ability of one or a few companies in an industry to set prices to serve their best interests. Because of lack of competition, such companies can, at least within a certain range, set a relatively high price in spite of weak consumer demand. This is often done to increase total profits, and it is particularly effective when consumer demand is relatively inelastic. Consequently, if one can show that the share of concentrated industries in the economy has been going up and that, at the same time, profit rates in such industries are higher than those in competitive industries, then at least some evidence supporting the monopoly-power hypothesis is established.

Evidence for this possible cause is presented by Anthony Scaperlanda (1977) and Howard Sherman (1976; 1977), while others discuss it as an explanation with high face value (Means et al. 1975; Belsley et al. 1976). Howard Sherman, for example, shows that in spite of recessionary pressures, prices of products offered by concentrated industries during the period from December 1973 to May 1975 rose 27 percent, while prices of products of nonconcentrated industries rose only 1.8 percent. Supporting this point of view, Scaperlanda shows that in past decades the market share of the 100 largest firms has been increasing. J. M. Blair even develops a model showing that "during periods of declining demand the expected behavior of oligopolistic prices will be the reverse of that assumed by traditional theory" (1974, p. 573). Finally, M. A. Okun (1977) cites prices that are determined by nonmarket forces—that is, administered prices—as one factor that, jointly with the rising cost of labor, is responsible for stagflation.

Labor Unions

Labor unions have a monopoly on labor. As a result they can obtain high wages for their members even when the demand for labor is weak, and thus contribute to stagflation (Hinshaw 1977; Means 1975; Parkins and Zis 1976; Prudy and Zis 1973, 1974; Scaperlanda 1977; Sherman 1977). However, Sherman dismisses this explanation by showing that during the 1973-75 recession aggregate real wages fell six points from their cycle peak; the monopolistic strength of labor unions, in terms of their share of the total labor force, has been declining; and the cost of labor per unit of production has been declining in recent years as a result of rising productivity (1977, p. 273).

On the other hand, wage increases won by labor unions in recent years and the cost-of-living adjustments are difficult to reject as possible stimulators of demand-pull inflation (inflation caused by too much money pursuing limited quantities of goods).

The Federal Government

The federal government may feed stagflation as a consumer, policy maker, and regulator.

As a consumer it often resorted to increasing tax rates so that increased revenues may be spent on products and services. However, Arthur Laffer (1979) has shown that increasing tax rates reduces the incentive to work, thus also reducing the government's revenues. In this situation, only a deficit budget will enable government to acquire goods and services, thus increasing demand-pull pressures.

As a policy maker the federal government may deepen stagflation by treating it as either an inflation or a recession, while in reality it is both. As a result economic, particularly monetary, policies during most of the 1970s often aggravated the problems rather than solving them.

Finally, as a regulator the federal government may contribute to higher prices by requiring producers to comply with costly regulations (such as those regarding air pollution) and by setting prices for products and services of regulated industries at levels higher than those achievable in situations of free competition (Kreinin 1975).

International Forces

The quadrupling of oil prices in 1974 by the OPEC cartel, and the price escalation of such other primary commodities as steel, cement, and copper; the frequent devaluation of the dollar; and frequent worldwide food shortages are cited by Kreinin (1975) as primary reasons for stagflation. According to at least one source the quadrupling of oil prices in 1974 is responsible for approximately one-third of American inflation. Furthermore, some researchers estimate that a rise of 15 percent in oil prices, such as that of

December 1978, generally contributes half a percentage point to the
rate of inflation (Parisi 1978).

While the impact of the above factors—oil prices, dollar devaluation, and food shortage—is somewhat similar to that of monopolistic powers, their being beyond the control of the American public
and its government indicates some degree of externally imposed
stagflation (Parkins and Zis 1976). Thus, the American economy
may experience stagflation in spite of its efforts to control it.

Secular Forces

Secular forces such as population change and inventions were
proposed by Hansen as possible causes of economic stagnation in
1939. According to his secular stagnation thesis, real economic
growth is normally brought about by an increase in investment or
capital formation. Investment, however, is determined by secular,
as opposed to economic, forces such as population growth; inventions, or at least innovations; and the discovery and development of
new resources and frontiers. In the absence of these investment-
inducing forces, economic growth comes to a halt, underemploy-
ment or unemployment develops, and there appears a widening gap
between potential GNP at full employment and actual GNP. These
developments signal the beginning of economic stagnation.

Hansen's thesis was developed in 1939 to explain the stagnating
American economy of the 1930s. The study of this thesis was minimized as World War II pulled the economy into a growth stage that
lasted, with minor interruptions, for more than three decades.
However, the economy that developed during the 1970s fits Hansen's
secular stagnation thesis surprisingly well.

The following discussion elaborates each component of Hansen's secular thesis in conjunction with the marketing implications
of stagflation.

Population Change

Population growth motivates capital formation and leads to
real economic growth because it represents an increasing total demand for products and services (Hansen 1939). Up to 60 percent of
the real economic growth in the United States and up to 50 percent
of that in Great Britain were attributed by Hansen to population
growth in the period 1850-1900. After World War II, however,
population growth in the United States declined steadily from an
annual rate of about 1.8 percent in the 1940s and 1950s, to 1.2 percent in the 1960s, to 0.8 percent in the 1970s. The downward trend

TABLE 1.1

Rate of Population Change by Age: Average Annual Percentage Change, 1940–2000

Year	Total	0–14 Years	15–29 Years	30–44 Years	45–64 Years	65 Years and Over
1940–1950	1.35	2.06	-.19	1.43	1.61	3.08
1950–1960	1.70	3.16	.11	.84	1.61	2.97
1960–1970	1.28	.41	3.40	-.40	1.49	1.94
1970–1980 (Series I)	1.05	-.67				
1970–1980 (Series II)	.92	-1.23	-2.11	2.18	.44	2.01
1970–1980 (Series III)	.81	-1.71				
1980–1990 (Series I)	1.32	2.64	-.92			
1980–1990 (Series II)	.95	1.26	-.96	2.91	.45	1.65
1980–1990 (Series III)	.67	-.01	-.98			
1990–2000 (Series I)	1.08	.74	1.27		2.5	
1990–2000 (Series II)	.69	.08	.08	.32		.56
1990–2000 (Series III)	.40	-.38	-.99			

Note: Series I assumes a fertility level of 2.7 children born per woman; Series II, 2.1 children; Series III, 1.7 children.

Source: U.S. Department of Commerce, Bureau of the Census, Current Population Reports, Series P-25, No. 601.

8

is yet to subside (Backman 1977; Economic Reports of the President 1976; World Bank 1978).

With the declining population growth there came a decline in capital formation; different age structure; changes in family size and attitudes toward marriage and family formation; and changes in the composition of the labor force and attitudes toward work life. Tables 1.1-1.3 present more details concerning population characteristics associated with population change. To marketers such changes have many implications (BusinessWeek 1976a); including the following:

Sales growth associated with population growth is on the decline (as in the case of baby furniture)
The elderly consumer group is growing and becoming a distinct market segment for food, housing, and personal services
The number of single-person households has increased dramatically, representing a lucrative market segment for housing and personal luxury goods and services
More and more women, including mothers of young children, have been entering the labor force, thus creating marketing opportunities for products such as convenience foods.

TABLE 1.2

Average Household Size and Single-Person Households
as Percent of All Households, 1955-75

	Average Size	Single-Person Households
1955	3.33	10.9
1960	3.33	13.1
1965	3.29	15.0
1970	3.14	17.1
1971	3.11	17.7
1972	3.06	18.3
1973	3.01	18.5
1974	2.97	19.1
1975	2.94	19.6

Source: U.S. Department of Commerce, Bureau of the Census, Current Population Report, Series P-20, No. 291.

TABLE 1.3

Average Annual Rate of Change of Population and Labor Force,
by Sex, 1950–55 to 1985–90

	1950–55	1955–60	1960–65	1965–70	1970–75	1975–80	1980–85	1985–90
Total population (all ages)	1.72	1.70	1.46	1.06	0.84	0.84	.99	.92
Total labor force (16 years and over)	1.28	1.16	1.35	2.14	1.97	1.81	1.29	.92
Male	.88	.57	.83	1.29	1.20	1.43	.92	.92
Female	2.23	2.46	2.40	3.70	3.23	2.38	1.84	1.24

Source: U.S. Department of Labor 1976; Bureau of Labor Statistics 1976.

Marketers are advised that in these situations, sales and product growth can be achieved by stimulating demand of a population that has been growing less rapidly and/or changing the marketing mix so as to appeal to the new population mix more effectively. To a large extent this was the general strategy of many marketers in the 1960s: demand stimulation ("more is better," "bigger is better") and various forms of market segmentation were used to increase profits by increasing sales and market share. Since then, however, changes in external forces such as inflation and recession have made this strategy less effective, if not counterproductive. (This point will be discussed more fully in Chapter 2.)

Innovation

Technological innovations are responsible for economic growth because they increase returns to labor and capital, and motivate investment and demand. Examples of such innovations and economic growth stimulators in the post-World War II period are the automobile industry; the multilevel interchange highway; the commercial aircraft industry; the synthetic fiber, plastics, new metal, electronics, and television industries; and the computer industry (Scaperlanda 1977). Technological and economic innovations, however, have declined because they have become more costly and risky while management's readiness to take risks has decreased sharply. As a result, total real expenditures for research and development—the source of most innovations—have declined more than 6 percent in the past decade (BusinessWeek 1976b). This, in turn, decreases the likelihood of future innovations, which are badly needed to stimulate economic growth. One may speculate, however, that future innovations that would move the American economy out of stagnation are those of solar technologies. Though there are many disagreements about the precise impacts of these innovations on society, Avraham Shama and Kenneth Jacobs (1979a, 1979b) claim that the future solar society would be markedly different than a society relying on conventional sources of energy.

For marketing and management, innovation is desirable because it may bring about drastic increases in sales, profits, and market share. Examples of such successful innovators are International Business Machines, Xerox, Texas Instruments, Minnesota Mining and Manufacturing, and Polaroid, which experienced rapid growth of sales and profits in 1945-74 (BusinessWeek 1976b). Yet, because true innovations are rather risky investments, the dominant strategy of many companies, including Bethlehem Steel, Du Pont, General Electric, General Foods, International Paper, and Procter and Gamble, is to invest in the less risky "me-too" products (such as mineral water, after Perrier's success) or to reposition old products (such as Arm and Hammer baking soda) to revive sales and profits (BusinessWeek 1976b).

Economic and War Frontiers

Economic frontiers are associated with the discovery and development of new resources and "lands." They make it possible to increase returns to labor and capital in the short and long runs. Examples of such frontiers are the settlement of the western United States and its impact on both the eastern and the western parts of the country; the space exploration efforts and their related technological change; and the development of the oil reserves at Prudhoe Bay, Alaska. This last development brought about a total investment of over $7.7 billion in the Alaska Pipeline, plus other investments made to take advantage of the demands of the Alaskan frontier (Scaperlanda 1977).

War frontiers, particularly when not in the homeland, stimulate investment in much the same manner. Though it is well known that wars are economic stimulators (and often overstimulators producing inflation), Hansen ignored this point and Scaperlanda (1977) attributed it to the secular stagnation thesis.

Of the two frontiers, the economic frontier is of particular importance to marketing management. It increases demand for products and services, leading to an increase in sales and profits in much the same manner as the impact of population growth. Marketers' behavior since 1960 has indicated a strong awareness of this point on a conceptual, though often intuitive, level. For example, as sales growth in the domestic markets slowed, management increased its marketing efforts abroad and international marketing began a period of rapid development.

Though Hansen's thesis was expressed decades ago, it is still applicable to the stagnant American and European economies. Consider the applications to the United States, England, Italy, France, Sweden, and many other industrialized countries that have been experiencing stagnant economic growth, that is, a growth well below past achievements and present potential. To marketing management Hansen's thesis indicates flattening disposable income, which results in flat and erratically changing demands for products and services.

A summary of Hansen's thesis and its applicability to the American economy of the 1960s and 1970s is presented in Table 1.4. As can be seen in this table, slow population growth, low rate of innovation, and the absence of economic (and war) frontiers led to a stagnant economy in the 1970s. On the other hand, the 1960s was a period of healthier economic growth: population increase, innovation, and economic frontiers were all rather high. These data seem to lend strong face validity to Hansen's arguments.

TABLE 1.4

Hansen's Thesis: American Economy, 1960s and 1970s

	1960s	1970s
Population growth[a] (percent)	1.2	0.8
and/or		
Innovation[b]	100.0	94.0
and/or		
Economic (and war) frontiers	many	few
determine		
Rate of economic growth[a] (percent)	4.3	2.5
resulting in	growth	stagnant
	economy	economy

[a]Average annual growth.
[b]Total budget for research and development is used as an indicator of innovation; 1968 is base year (100.0).
Source: Adapted from World Bank 1978; data on innovation reported by National Science Foundation.

Nevertheless, Hansen's view of stagnation disregarded a very important factor of the 1970s economy: the coexistence of inflation and a stagnant rate of economic growth. Even those who explained and expanded Hansen's thesis followed his disinterest in the inflationary factor, or dismissed it as "unlikely" (Higgins 1950; see also Scaperlanda 1977). Although theoretically an unlikely situation, the simultaneous occurrence of inflation and stagnation has become the reality of most industrialized countries since 1973.

The study of this economic environment labeled by Hansen as "stagnation" in 1939 was revised by the Economist in the 1970s and termed "stagflation" to describe a stagnant economy during periods of inflation (Griffiths 1976). Some also refer to it as "growth recession," meaning an economy characterized by a very low growth (2-3 percent), which results in unemployment, weak income and demand, and an idle production capacity.

In conclusion, although secular forces constitute partial causes of stagflation, so do other forces: monopoly power, labor unions, the federal government, and international forces. Taken together, they explain the stagflation phenomenon more fully even if not completely.

A summary of stagflation in terms of inflation and unemployment is presented in Table 1.5.

TABLE 1.5

Stagflation: Inflation and Unemployment Rates, 1970-79

Year	Inflation Rate (percent)	Unemployment Rate (percent)
1970	5.9	4.9
1971	4.3	5.9
1972	3.3	5.6
1973	6.2	4.9
1974	11.0	5.6
1975	9.9	8.5
1976	5.8	7.7
1977	6.5	7.0
1978	9.0	5.8
1979	13 (est.)	5.6-5.8

Source: Compiled by the author.

SCOPE AND DEPTH

Stagflation became a worldwide phenomenon in the 1970s, undoubtedly the most significant economic and social phenomenon since the Great Depression. Serious degrees of inflation and recession affected Canada, England, France, Italy, the United States, and many other nations. Familiar Keynesian remedies were ineffective, leaving business and government policy makers helpless. Furthermore, stagflation cut deeply through many facets of life.

Ever since Hansen's secular stagnation thesis (1939), more and more authorities—economists—have attributed the occurrence of stagflation to noneconomic (secular) forces. While Hansen attributed stagnation to the absence of such secular forces as population growth, innovations, and new economic frontiers, Parkins and

Zis (1976), Avraham Shama (1978), and J. A. Trevithick (1977) have argued that stagflation is basically a social phenomenon. For example, Trevithick argues that fundamental sources of stagflation "have nothing to do with basically economic factors but rather they are primarily the result of sociological and political forces . . ." (1977, p. 13). Following this point of view, Fred Hirsch (1978) postulates that stagflation results from the fact that in the past, society became accustomed to high rates of material growth. However, because the expected rate of such a growth is below past performance, the outcome is frustration and an increasing attention to distribution—to the division of the pie rather than to growth (see also Meadows et al. 1972; Robinson 1976).

Thus, deceptively starting as a new economic force, stagflation quickly became the number-one consumer, business, social, and political issue. Many facets of life, numerous business decisions, and important political moves are strongly affected by stagflation. As an indication of such saliency, one may cite the increasing media coverage of stagflation as a major item, and the growing number of polls designed to measure the impact of the economic environment on society.

CURES

On the macro level it is clear that stagflation cannot be treated effectively by Keynesian remedies, that is, by expanding or contracting fiscal and monetary policies. Keynesian remedies are prescribed to work against either inflation or unemployment (recession), because theoretically they occur separately. Therefore, such remedies are totally ineffective when applied to economies experiencing both inflation and unemployment simultaneously. Consequently a noninflationary economic growth policy is required to curtail stagflation.

The various TIP (tax-based income policies) plans, including Phase II of President Jimmy Carter's economic policy, are examples of such noninflationary growth policies (Okun 1977; Wallich 1978). President Carter's economic policy, for example, placed an annual ceiling of 7 percent increase on average wages, and a ceiling of 5.75 percent increase on average prices. Thus, allowing prices of goods and services, and the price of labor, to go up only moderately curbs inflation, and at the same time may stimulate a moderate rate of growth or productivity. This is in keeping with prescriptions arguing that in an era of stagflation, "Both money supply and wages must behave themselves. For prosperity, money must adjust to wages. For price stability, average wages must rise only with productivity" (Lerner 1977a, p. 387).

Nevertheless, the TIP plans treat stagflation as an economic phenomenon only. However, since stagflation is to some extent a social phenomenon caused by secular forces, it is too optimistic to expect that economic measures alone can cure it. Consequently, if an effective antistagflation policy is to be made, some measures should be directed to dealing with its secular causes.

To marketers stagflation is a paradoxical external power requiring business policies designed to achieve expansion and contraction concurrently, so as to achieve profit and sales goals. This difficult situation is compounded by the fact that the rates of inflation, unemployment, and demand have been changing quickly and unpredictably. Yet, marketing managers are not totally helpless in these conditions. Chapter 2 outlines a framework designed to help management deal with stagflation effectively.

THEORETICAL FRAMEWORK

Changes in the economic environment affect both business and consumers. As long as such changes follow a definable trend and are relatively easy to predict, both business and consumers can easily adjust to them, and often take advantage of them. Such was the case between the end of World War II and 1973. The economy enjoyed rapid and meaningful growth, and the rates of inflation and unemployment were rather low. Marketing management enjoyed real and rapid growth in terms of sales, profits, and expansion, and thus became accustomed to a rapid and positive pace. Consumers also enjoyed real and rapid growth in terms of disposable income, consumption, and product selection.

Beginning with the oil shortage of 1973, stagflation—a radically different and less predictable economic state—appeared. This left both business and consumers uncertain as to how to respond and adjust.

The conceptual framework of this book is presented in Figure 1.2. As depicted, changes in the economic environment—shortage, inflation, recession, and various types of stagflation (box I)—affect both business and the consumers (boxes II and III). As a result of such influences, business management and consumers develop new strategies and tactics to cope with the new economic climates (boxes IV and V). Thus, for example, in an era of shortage, business management may utilize a strategy to reduce demand—that is, a demarketing strategy—while in a climate of recession it may utilize a strategy designed to stimulate demand. Similarly, consumers facing shortage might start hoarding, and save less when they experience inflation.

FIGURE 1.2

A Conceptual Framework of the Relationships among the
Economic Environment, Business, and Consumers

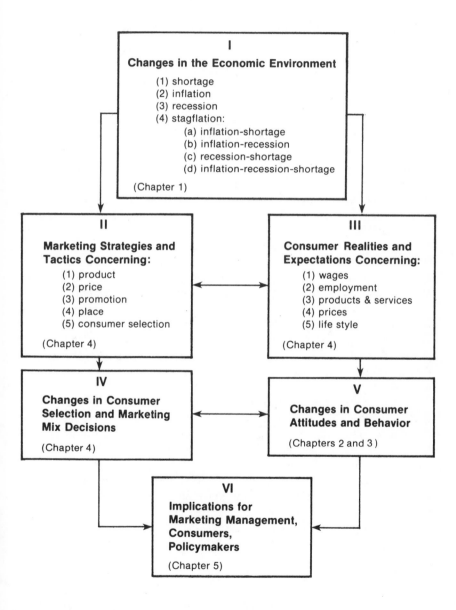

Source: Constructed by the author.

The net result of such adjustments by business management and the consumers is a net change in the relationships between them in terms of prices, products and product assortment, credit conditions, promotional appeals, and places of selling and purchasing. In turn, this change in the business-consumer relationship represents new and possibly more profitable opportunities to marketing management, and indicates coping strategies for both consumers and policy makers (box VI).

Stagflation and Business

It is unquestionable that stagflation affects most business decisions. Decisions concerning investment, expansion, diversification, personnel, product line, pricing, promotion, and even distribution are affected by management perceptions of the impact of stagflation. Yet, because stagflation is a novel economic phenomenon, management is often confused about how to deal with it. For example, is stagflation a form of inflation? of recession? of shortage? a combination of all such forces?

The answers to these questions are crucial because they define the nature of stagflation and indicate coping strategies to management. For instance, if it is decided that stagflation and inflation are equivalent, then a general expansion strategy to maintain consumer demand and profits is in order. Such a strategy may include the following tactics: adjusting prices and credit policies frequently, shortening product line, offering product substitutes, and temporarily using demarketing promotion. However, if it is decided that stagflation is equivalent to recession, then the above measures are dysfunctional.

To complicate the matter further, it is proposed in this book that stagflation is any combination of inflation, recession, and shortage. This, in turn, puts management in a very difficult position, in that anything done to cope with one of the stagflation components (such as inflation) may increase the negative impact of another (such as recession). Consequently, trade-off analysis of the impact of the two components may have to be carried out. (A detailed discussion of this concept and its impact on marketing management appear in Chapter 2.)

Stagflation and Society

Stagflation breeds a new type of consumer, whose reactions to the business environment are markedly different from and less predictable than those of the prestagflation consumer. As a result, business—which in the 1960s became accustomed to stimulating demand as the main mode of stimulating profits—may suddenly have to spend more energy on product-line development and pruning, consumer selection, and competitive strategy. Furthermore, stagflation may require that at least some businesses or industries formulate policies to reduce demand rather than stimulate it that is, demarketing)—exactly the opposite of past conditioning.

Perhaps the most important social outcome results from the fact that stagflation indicates slow growth of the national pie—much too slow relative to people's expectations and previous conditioning. Having gotten used to rapidly improving standards of living, families suddenly face a halt to upward economic and social mobility. Furthermore, as the socioeconomic expectations of the post-World War II period materialized, expectations—particularly those of the middle class—increased much more. In this condition rising expectations for affluence can be satisfied only if increases in real income become more substantial.

Such, however, is not the case during stagflation. The pie, in real terms, grows very slowly during any type of stagflation. Consequently the various social groups must compete to get a greater share of the pie, which has been shrinking relative to expectations. In addition, since middle-class expectations, in comparison with those of the lower class, are much higher relative to attainable share of the pie, the result is struggle to realize at least some aspirations. This militancy is further reinforced by middle-class perceptions of the gains of the semiskilled and blue-collar workers. These perceptions help to increase the squeeze felt by the middle class and to increase its outspokenness, militancy, or "revolt." (Detailed discussions of the impact of stagflation on consumers and society are presented in Chapters 3 and 4.)

Stagflation and Economic Policy

Since stagflation is any combination of inflation, recession, and shortage, economic policy makers may be confronted with different types of stagflation that affect different segments of the economy differently. Therefore, if effective coping policies are to be made, different measures must be prescribed for the different segments. For example, it may well be that some segments require expansionary measures, while others need contracting measures. This, however, requires increased intervention by the federal government in the economy. It also hampers the principle of treating the various economic segments equally.

Nevertheless, though not clearly stated, government policies, beginning with "jawboning" and ending with Carter's Phase II economic policy, are directed toward more specially tailored intervention.

In this chapter the causes and cures of stagflation have been discussed, and its impact on business and consumers outlined. Stagflation has been shown to be much more complex than was previously thought. Accordingly, there may be several types of stagflation that affect various facets of life differently, consumer and business decisions differently, and require different coping strategies by consumers, management, and policy makers.

REFERENCES

Backman, J. 1977. "Economic Growth or Stagnation: An Overview." Address in Key Issues lecture series. New York University School of Business and Public Administration, October 19.

Belsley, D. A., E. J. Kane, P. A. Samuelson, and R. M. Saldow. 1976. Inflation, Trade and Taxes. Columbus: Ohio State University Press.

Blair, J. M. 1974. "Market Power and Inflation: A Short Run Target Return Model." Journal of Economic Issues 8 (June): 453-74.

BusinessWeek. 1976a. "How the Changing Age Mix Changes Markets." January 12: 74-78.

BusinessWeek. 1976b. "The Breakdown of U.S. Innovation." February 16: 56-68.

Economic Reports of the President. 1976. Washington, D.C.: U.S. Government Printing Office.

Friedman, I. S. 1973. Inflation: A Worldwide Disaster. Boston: Houghton, Mifflin.

Friedman, M. 1977. "Nobel Lecture: Inflation and Unemployment." Journal of Political Economy 85 (June): 451-72.

Griffiths, B. 1976. Inflation: The Price of Prosperity. New York: Holmes and Meier.

Hansen, A. H. 1939. "Economic Progress and Declining Population Growth." American Economic Review 29, no. 1: 1-5.

Higgins, B. 1948. "Concepts and Criteria of Secular Stagnation." In Income, Employment and Public Policy: Essays in Honor of Alvin H. Hansen, edited by B. Higgins. New York: W. W. Norton.

_____. 1950. "The Concept of Secular Stagnation." American Economic Review 40 (March): 159-66.

Hinshaw, R., ed. 1977. Stagflation: An International Problem. New York: Marcel Dekker.

Hirsch, F. 1978. Social Limits to Growth. Cambridge, Mass.: Harvard University Press.

Howard, J. V. 1976. "Methods of Controlling Inflation." Economic Journal 86 (December): 832-44.

Kaldor, N. 1976. "Inflation and Recession in the World Economy." Economic Journal 86 (December): 703-14.

Keynes, J. M. 1936. The General Theory of Employment, Interest, and Money. London: Macmillan.

Kreinin, M. 1975. "Inflation, Recession and Stagflation." MSU Business Topics 23 (Winter): 5-18.

Laffer, Arthur. 1979. "To Set the Economy Right." Time, August 27, pp. 24-36.

Lerner, A. P. 1977a. "Stagflation—Its Causes and Cure." Challenge 20 (September-October): 14-19.

_____. 1977b. "From Pre-Keynes to Post-Keynes." Social Research 44: 387-415.

Levinson, Charles. 1971. Capital, Inflation and the Multinationals. New York: Macmillan.

Mallen, B. 1977. "More General View of Inflation: Lessons of the Mid-70's." Business Quarterly 42 (Spring): 35-43.

Meadows, D. H., et al. 1972. The Limits to Growth. New York: Universe Books.

Means, Gardiner C., et al. 1975. The Roots of Inflation. New York: Burt Franklin.

Okun, M. A. 1975a. Equity and Efficiency: The Big Trade-Off. Washington, D.C.: Brookings Institution.

_____. 1975b. "A Postmorten of the 1974 Recession." Brookings Staff Paper on Economic Activity. Washington, D.C.: Brookings Institution.

_____. 1977. "The Great Stagflation Swamp." Brookings Staff Papers on Economic Activity. Washington, D.C.: Brookings Institution.

Parisi, J. A. 1978. "OPEC Action: Effects on U.S." New York Times, December 15, p. D1.

Parkins, M., and G. Zis, eds. 1976. Inflation in Open Economies. Manchester: Manchester University Press.

Phillips, A. W. 1958. "The Relationship between Unemployment and the Rate of Change of Money Wage Rates in the U.K. 1861-1957." Economica n.s. 25, no. 100: 283-99.

Prudy, D. L., and G. Zis. 1973. "Trade Unions and Wage Inflation in the U.K.: A Reappraisal." In Essays in Modern Economics, edited by J. M. Markin. London: Longmans.

_____. 1974. "On the Concept Measurement of Union Militancy." In Inflation and Labor Markets, edited by D. Laidler and D. L. Prudy, pp. 38-60. Manchester: Manchester University Press.

Purchasing. 1973. "The Supply Squeeze Is Worldwide." October 2, pp. 19-20.

Reese, J. 1977. "The New Inflation." Journal of Economic Issues 9 (June): 285-97.

Robinson, J. 1976. "The Age of Growth." Challenge 19 (May-June): 4-9.

Santomero, A. M., and J. J. Seater. 1978. "The Inflation Unemployment Trade off: A Critique of the Literature." Journal of Economic Literature 16 (June): 499-544.

Scaperlanda, A. 1977. "Hansen's Secular Stagnation Thesis Once Again." Journal of Economic Issues 11, no. 2 (June): 223-43.

Shama, Avraham. 1978. "Marketing Management and the Consumer during Periods of Stagflation." Journal of Marketing 42, no. 3 (July): 43-52.

Shama, A., and K. Jacobs. 1979a. Solar Energy Policy: The Policymaker and the Advocate. Golden, Colo.: Solar Energy Research Institute.

_____. 1979b. "Solar Energy: What Is It That We Are Expected to Be Confident About?" The Denver Post, August 17, p. 18.

Sherman, H. J. 1976. Stagflation: A Radical Theory of Unemployment and Inflation. New York: Harper and Row.

_____. 1977. "Monopoly Power and Stagflation." Journal of Economic Issues 11, no. 2 (June): 269-84.

Silk, L. 1976. "The 'Secular Slowdown' Thesis." New York Times, October 21, pp. 55, 59.

Trevithick, J. A. 1977. Inflation: A Guide to the Crisis in Economics. New York: Penguin Books.

U.S. Bureau of Labor Statistics. 1976. "New Labor Force Projections to 1990." Monthly Labor Review (December).

U.S. Department of Commerce, Bureau of the Census. Current Population Reports, ser. P-25, no. 601.

_____. 1971. 1970 Census of Population. Washington, D.C.: U.S. Government Printing Office.

_____. Current Population Reports, ser. P-20, no. 291.

U.S. Department of Labor. 1976. Employment and Training Report of the President. Washington, D.C.: U.S. Government Printing Office.

Wallich, H. 1978. "Stabilization Goals: Balancing Inflation and Unemployment." American Economic Review Papers and Proceedings 69 (May): 159-64.

World Bank. 1978. World Development Indicators. June.

2
MARKETING IN A
STAGFLATION ECONOMY

Four types are identified and discussed in the present chapter, following Avraham Shama's (1978) taxonomy. The implications of each type for management in general and for marketing management in particular are discussed in detail.

STAGFLATION AND BASIC ECONOMIC FORCES

Stagflation has been commonly regarded as a stagnant economy in a period of inflation (see, for example, Griffiths 1976; Kelley and Scheewe 1975; Lerner 1977a, 1977b; Okun 1977; Sherman 1977). Refining this definition, Shama (1978) argues that it represents any combination of three basic forces: shortage, inflation, and recession. Accordingly, one can identify inflation-shortage, inflation-recession, recession-shortage, and inflation-recession-shortage. The main difference between each of the basic forces and any of the above combinations is that while each force influences the economy in one direction, each combination influences the economy in different, often diametrically opposing, directions. For example, while inflation represents a consistent process of rising prices and recession represents a consistent process of weakening demand, the

Portions of this chapter are adapted from the author's article, "Management and Consumers in an Era of Stagflation," Journal of Marketing 42, no. 3 (July 1978): 43-52, by permission of the American Marketing Association.

inflation-recession combination represents an economy experiencing contradictory pressures of rising and weakening demand simultaneously. Steel, aluminum, and fibers are three major industries operating in this type of stagflation.

Because shortage, inflation, and recession are the foundations of all types of stagflation, a discussion of each is necessary before one proceeds to the various types of stagflation. Since these three forces are discussed in economic and marketing literature, only a short review of the most relevant points, and some examples, follow.

BASIC ECONOMIC CLIMATES

Shortages

Shortage is an economic and psychological state that occurs when the demand is greater than the supply at the existing price level. Both business, as a consumer of raw materials, and consumers of final products have experienced various degrees of shortage—real or contrived—since 1973: oil, coffee, natural gas, aluminum, cement, copper, textiles, and lumber. Inconsistent with the Keynesian model, a rise in price and a decrease in demand were not the only factors operating in a shortage environment. Psychological factors and expectations exerted an influence as well. For example, in the deep and widely manifested shortages of 1973 and 1974, consumers not only expected higher prices for products in short supply but also expected more shortages, were ready to pay even higher prices, were ready to spend more time and energy to obtain products in short supply, increased their inventory of those products by hoarding, and in general became more pessimistic about the economy and the country.

The main roles of marketing management in a period of shortages are demarketing in the short run and marketing and consumer-mix modifications in the longer run. More specifically, marketing management is advised to consider the following adaptive activities in shortage situations (see, for example, Cullwick 1975; Hanna, Kizinibash, and Smart 1975; Kelley and Scheewe 1975; Kotler 1974; Nekvasil 1974; Weiss 1974):

Change the product mix by narrowing the product line according to profitability criteria, reducing the content of scarce materials in the end product, increasing research on and development of scarce materials, and introducing substitute products for scarce goods

Adjust prices to maintain profitability and tighten credit to discourage marginal accounts

Change distribution to make the scarce products less available (small order policy, withdrawal from marginal territories, and reducing the number of operating hours, for example)

Decrease promotion of scarce goods and change their appeal, while increasing the promotion of more readily available products.

Examples of adjustment to a scarcity or shortage situation include the following:

> In its pursuit to maintain profitability in an era of shortages, General Electric Co., for example, has dropped fans, blenders, humidifiers, and vacuum cleaners, and as the price of zinc increased by more than 300% in one year, GE became certain to develop new materials for its stand mixer.
> Similarly, Philco-Ford Corp. has chopped half of its color-TV screen sizes, and over one-third of its refrigerator models (BusinessWeek 1974e).

Also, as consumers turned away from coffee when shortage caused its price to rise sky-high, the major coffee roasters and packers turned to a cheaper substitute, chicory, and offered blends of coffee containing that ingredient.

When the shortage subsides, the marketing mix must be changed accordingly. Staying with the coffee example, as the shortage began to ease:

> General Foods cut the wholesale price of a 1-lb. can of Maxwell House coffee by 20¢ resulting in a selling price of $3.21. Furthermore, General Foods plans gradual price changes totaling 25% in one year (BusinessWeek 1977).

Changes made in response to shortages may affect the consumers and their loyalty to the company. Marketing management should carry out those marketing-mix changes that help achieve long-run profitability and consumer satisfaction. To do so, it must research its target markets and investigate how the various modifications of the marketing mix will affect them. This, in turn, will enable management to select its target markets and choose an optimal marketing mix in a period of shortages (Kotler 1973).

Inflation

Inflation is characterized by rising prices of raw materials and final products and services. Depending on what triggers such a process, economists normally distinguish between two types of inflation: demand-pull inflation, which is characterized by full employment and too much money chasing too few goods and services; and cost-push inflation, due to rising costs of raw materials and production, and characterized by production overcapacity and varying degrees of unemployment.

The basic role of marketing management in such inflationary situations is efficient control of production, selling costs, and consumer demand. Within a certain range, demand stimulation in a cost-push inflation is essential; otherwise a full-scale recession may develop. Keeping costs down so that prices do not have to be raised drastically because of excessive demand or higher costs will bring about a profitable level of demand. Simultaneously, marketing management must orient itself toward innovative production, selling, and consumer satisfaction possibilities that can improve both profitability and consumer satisfaction. More specifically, the following activities are open to consideration by marketing management confronted with inflation:

1. Study how inflation affects the target consumers of each of the company's products. It is logical to expect that different target consumers are affected differently; thus various degrees of modifications of the marketing mix are called for.

2. Keep all costs down. Effective control of costs enables the company to maintain profitability even when it raises prices only moderately. However, success in keeping costs and prices down may become a disadvantage if the relatively low price creates an excess demand that the company cannot fill quickly, to the satisfaction of all consumers. Another possibility is that the relatively low price achieved by efficient management may be associated by consumers and/or by competitors' promotion with low quality, which may result in a decreased demand. Consequently, controlling costs to keep the price down should be carefully managed, in order to avoid negative effects.

3. Emphasize profit margins. In an inflation economy, marginal costs normally are very high. In this situation profit maximization can be achieved more readily by emphasizing profit margins than by maximization of sales volume. In a demand-pull inflation this may mean that not increasing sales, or even selling less, can increase the company's profitability. On the other

hand, in a cost-push inflation a moderate, rather than drastic, increase in sales may mean greater profitability.

4. Flexible price policy and frequent adjustment of prices are essential. An examination of the cost and price structure every 90 days became the norm among most major corporations. Raising prices in anticipation of inflation is another common behavior. In addition, changing the cost-accounting method from FIFO (first in, first out) to LIFO (last in, first out) offers some short-run advantages that Du Pont, Radio Corporation of America, Dow Chemical, Reynolds Metals, Texaco, and more than 200 other major corporations have adopted (Forbes 1975).

5. Maintenance of competitive pricing. In a period of rising prices, most consumers attach greater importance to price, and a company not able to maintain a competitive price may experience faltering demand.

6. Periodic reexamination of accounts and territories in terms of performance criteria acceptable to the company, so as to make sound judgments concerning their retention. Dropping marginal accounts and territories—when legally possible and when it does not alienate other, more profitable, accounts and territories—may be a sound policy in a period of inflation. An examination of potential accounts and territories—particularly in a cost-pull inflation—in terms of the same criteria may bring in additional satisfactory accounts and/or territories.

7. Innovate. In a period of inflation, innovation may be particularly rewarding. Thus, innovation in production technology can bring about higher productivity that can help to keep costs down; product innovation may enable the company to offer the consumer a product substitute that costs less; a product innovation may enable the company to offer a new, more consumer-satisfying product; logistic innovation may make it cheaper to get the product to the consumer, thus controlling cost and price; and innovation can frequently prevent the customer from making price comparisons by creating a differentiated product.

Whether any of the above steps is taken in a period of inflation depends on marketing management's perception of the type, rate, and duration of inflation, and the degree to which its products and target consumers are affected. One can logically assume that different markets are influenced differently, and that different companies therefore require different adaptive mixes.

Here is how one company changes its marketing mix—or, more particularly, its product mix—in pursuit of profitability in a period of inflation.

Sun Oil's division of Lubrication and Metalworking
materials has cut its metalworking oils from 1,150
grades to 92, its lubes from 1,000 grades to 200,
and its greases from 225 to 29. This product-line
pruning has increased productivity by 20%-30% as it
drastically reduced kettle-cleaning time in the plant
(BusinessWeek 1974e).

Recession

Recession is a process of decreasing demand for raw materials, and services (including labor). A lower demand for labor
means a smaller disposable income, which further decreases demand. In essence, recession is demand-push inflation in reverse:
decreasing demand and, in general, a very slow or contracting
economy. Socially, recession is accompanied by an increasing degree of pessimism and a tendency to blame business and government.

The basic step that marketing management should take in response to such a process is to reexamine its marketing mix and its
target consumers, in order to discover effective and efficient ways
to stimulate the weakening demand. More specifically, an examination of the following points constitutes an important part of a sound
antirecession strategy:

1. Reexamination of target consumers. A recession may influence
    consumers in such a way that a change in the definition of the
    target groups may be necessary. Thus, redefining the target
    group alone can improve the company's performance. Equally
    important is the influence of recession on consumers' attitudes
    and expectations. A pessimistic outlook may be more harmful
    to the company in the long run than the faltering demand for its
    products.
2. Reexamination of the product line and the product line can
    show the company how well the various models are selling and
    what features are more positively evaluated by consumers.
    This can help the company introduce changes in the product
    line and product features. Introducing cheaper, more functional models while "shortening" the top of the product line may
    be a sound antirecession step.
3. Reexamination of price structure. Changing price differentials
    among the various products may increase total sales and profits.
    General price cutting may also bring about increases in sales
    (and even profits). However, the marketer should be aware that

such change may influence consumers' image of his products negatively.

4. Revitalization of demand by increasing promotion. Traditionally the promotion budget is determined as a percentage of last year's sales or of expected sales. This means that it shrinks in a recession—exactly when an increased promotion budget could increase sales.

5. Reexamination of the physical distribution system. In a depressed economy the individual firm can increase its sales by decreasing the number of levels in the distribution process. For example, offering the product directly to the consumer or eliminating some of the middlemen can enable the company to lower the price to the consumer and also increase its sales and profits. This strategy may antagonize the eliminated middlemen and influence those who are left negatively. Therefore, in decreasing the number of levels of distribution, the company should compare short-run and long-run gains and losses from such a decision.

6. Reexamination of credit market, rates, and structure so as to reduce costs.

7. Examination of new marketing opportunities. Recession represents a new economic climate that can offer new and profitable opportunities. Do-it-yourself products, generic products, and L-A (limited assortment) stores are but a few examples.

The housing industry of 1975 is an excellent example of the role of marketing management in a recession.

Faced with growing uncertainty and slow growing disposable income on the one hand, and the rising cost of private homes on the other, many potential buyers left the housing market. To cope with this situation of radically declining demand, many builders adjusted their marketing mix by offering smaller, cheaper houses. Miami-based Deltona Corp., for example, has downgraded its entire product line in 1975. Whereas Deltona offered homes in the $30,000 to $56,000 range up to 1975, the new product line was in the $17,800 to $30,000 range (BusinessWeek 1975c).*

---

*Reprinted from the April 14, 1975, issue of BusinessWeek by special permission, (c) 1975 by McGraw-Hill, Inc., New York, N.Y., 10020. All rights reserved.

A fuller and more formal listing of adaptive strategies and tactics to be considered by marketing management during periods of inflation, recession, and shortage is presented in Table 2.1.

TYPES OF STAGFLATION

The four types of stagflation—inflation-shortage, inflation-recession, recession-shortage, and inflation-recession-shortage—are similar in that each of them represents a combination of two or more basic economic forces; they call for innovation, increased productivity, and diversification so as to reduce costs or improve profitability; and they emphasize the importance of consumer research for the purpose of determining effective marketing strategy and marketing-mix tactics. Yet, each represents a unique economic state that calls for unique adjustment measures.

Inflation-Shortage

Inflation-shortage includes components that to some degree reinforce each other. Inflation is characterized by rising prices of products and services. The occurrence of shortages in this state may further increase the gap between supply and demand, and push prices up. This state can be economy-wide, as was the case in 1974, or it can occur—at least in the short run—in specific industries.

As can be seen in Table 2.1, both inflation and shortages call for an overall strategy of demand reduction and almost identical marketing-mix tactics. Therefore, the inflation-shortage combination can be conceptually treated as an inflation that affects the industries and consumers experiencing shortages more severely. Consequently, a company operating in an environment of inflation-shortages must assess the influence of inflation and of shortages on consumer demand for its products. The company can then proceed to develop an adaptive strategy designed to reduce or regulate demand and/or to redefine its target groups. Fortunately, whatever strategy is chosen will have some effectiveness in meeting both situations.

Because different industries are differently influenced by inflation-shortage, one can logically expect a need for different levels of adjustment. This means that an economy experiencing inflation and shortages must be treated on an industry-by-industry basis, and within each industry on a company-by-company and product-by-product basis. Valid generalizations cannot be made

TABLE 2.1

Adaptive Strategies and Tactics in Periods of Shortages, Inflation, and Recession

Strategy/ Tactics	Shortages	Inflation	Recession
	Demand reduction in the short run and demand adjustment in the long run	Demand reduction	Demand increase
Product	Narrow product line Offer cheaper, more functional products Purchase scarce materials more carefully and strategically Make scarce material go further Invest in researching substitute materials Introduce substitute products Avoid quantity discount	Shorten product line Offer cheaper, more functional products Purchase raw material more carefully and strategically Use less expensive (or lower-grade) material in production Invest in researching substitute materials Avoid quantity discount	Narrow product line Offer cheaper, more functional products and/or cut top of product line Use less raw materials in production Offer quantity discount
Price	Raise prices Adjust prices periodically (upward) Change price differential among products in the line Stop price discounting Tighten credit Centralize price decisions	Raise prices Adjust prices frequently (upward) Change price differential products in the line to decrease total demand Stop price discounting Tighten credit Centralize price decisions	Lower prices when possible Change price differential to increase total demand Offer price discount Loosen credit Centralize price decisions

Promotion	Demarket through promotion / Decrease promotion of scarce goods / Increase promotion of more readily available products	Demarket through promotion / Decrease promotion via advertising and personal selling / Push the more profitable products	Remarket through promotion / Increase promotion to stimulate demand / Cultivate every potential account and territory / Motivate sales force to sell more
Place	Limit quantity per customer / Limit distribution to make products less available	Limit quantity per customer / Limit distribution to make product less available / Utilize a higher price to achieve product differentiation	Increase distribution outlets / Motivate middlemen to buy more of the product and push it / Offer products directly to consumers
Consumer	Study how consumers and potential consumers are affected / Drop marginal accounts when possible / Treat consumers so as to maximize loyalty	Study how consumers and potential consumers are affected / Drop marginal accounts when possible / Treat consumers so as to maximize loyalty	Study how consumers and potential consumers are affected / Cultivate even marginally profitable accounts / Treat consumers so as to maximize sales
	Innovate / Increase productivity / Diversify	Innovate / Increase productivity / Diversify	Innovate / Increase productivity / Diversify

Source: Compiled by the author.

before substantial knowledge is derived from the study and experience of inflation-shortage. For example, faced with shortages and inflation in the travel industry, most major airlines offered cheaper products (charter flights) and fewer scheduled flights. On the other hand, Samsonite decided to change its product concept, market segmentation, and promotion strategies. Women were to be offered fashionable, lightweight luggage while men were to be offered durability and capacity. And, to meet consumer demand for economy in a scarcity situation and to overcome price resistance:

> General Motors Corp. has recently stripped down nine
> of its small car models, eliminating among other
> things, four-speed transmissions, and steel belted
> tires from the list of standard equipment. These
> product changes made it possible for GM to chop as
> much as 8% of the list price (BusinessWeek 1974c).

Inflation-Recession

An economic environment experiencing both inflation and recession is paradoxical, in that inflation and recession call for diametrically opposing adjustment strategies and many incongruent tactics. As one can see from Table 2.1, inflation calls for a strategy to reduce demand while recession calls for a strategy to increase demand. However, as Arthur Burns—at the time the chairman of the Federal Reserve—put it: ". . . demand can be increased to fight unemployment, or reduced to fight inflation, but . . . demand can't be simultaneously increased and decreased to fight both unemployment and inflation" (Silk 1976). Consistent with this, and except for similarities in product tactics, inflation-recession calls for incongruent, if not contradictory, marketing-mix tactics. Thus inflation utilizes tactics of raising prices and dropping less profitable accounts, reducing promotion, and tightening credit, while recession utilizes tactics of cutting prices or changing their structure, increasing promotion, loosening credit, and widening distribution.

How can marketing management handle such an economic climate of contradictory pressures? One should first recognize that while the general economy experiences a given mix of inflation and recession, different industries, different companies, and even different products within a given industry or company may be experiencing different mixes of such climates. Consequently, what may be an effective strategy to cope with an inflation-recession mix on the national or on an industry level may be far less effective, and possibly even damaging, on the single-company or single-product level. That is, the most effective anti-inflation-recession mix is company-specific and product-specific. Each company is confronted with a specific trade-off matrix of anti-inflation and anti-recession measures. The more the company employs anti-inflation measures, the more severe the effects of recession become.

As can be seen from Figure 2.1, a company confronted with inflation-recession may treat it solely as an inflation environment, and thus take an optimal level of anti-inflation measures. This is indicated by point A in Figure 2.1. However, point A also means that the company is completely ignoring recessionary pressures, and thus is not reacting to declining demand. The contrary is represented by point B: an optimal level of anti-recession measures and a total disregard of the inflation environment. Thus points A and B represent optimal responses to a pure environment of inflation and a pure environment of recession, respectively. Any meaningful treatment of an inflation-recession environment is represented on $\overline{AB}$. Once this is realized, the company has to investigate the rate of exchange between anti-inflationary and anti-recessionary measures. This rate may be constant or variable.

FIGURE 2.1

The Trade-off Matrix between Anti-Inflation
and Anti-Recession Measures

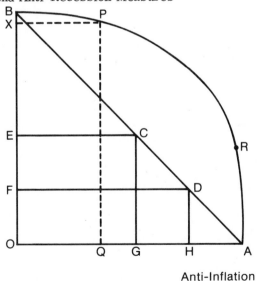

Source: Constructed by the author.

A constant rate of exchange—such as the case on $\overline{ADCB}$—means that for every unit of anti-inflation measures, one must give up a fixed amount of anti-recession measures. For example, to increase the anti-inflation measures from O to G, one must decrease the level of anti-recession measures from B to E; and to further increase such measures from G to H, one has to decrease the level of anti-recession measures from E to F. The "price" paid for moving any one unit from O to H in terms of giving up anti-recession measures is constant.

On the other hand, a variable rate of exchange, illustrated by points $\overline{ARPB}$, means that the "price" of additional measures of anti-inflation strategy in terms of anti-recession measures varies according to the specific mix from which one starts. For example, starting from point B, the "price" of anti-inflation measures is relatively very low. One pays a marginal reduction in the level of anti-recession measures ($\overline{BX}$) for a relatively big anti-inflation measure ($\overline{OQ}$). However, as one increases the anti-inflation measures in the mix, the "price" paid in terms of abandoning anti-recession measures goes up. This notion of a variable rate of exchange between the two measures seems to represent reality more accurately, and therefore the company must try to quantify such trade-offs before arriving at an optimal anti-inflation-recession strategy mix.

The anti-inflation and anti-recession trade-off mix is determined by many factors. Some of these are listed below:

Impact (or rate) of inflation. The greater the impact of inflation on the company, the lower the "price" the company pays for anti-inflation measures in terms of giving up anti-recession measures

Impact (or rate) of recession. The greater the impact of recession, the lower the "price" the company pays for anti-recession measures in terms of anti-inflation steps

Elasticity of demand for the company product(s). Relatively inelastic demand may allow the company to utilize an adjustment mix containing relatively more anti-inflation tactics (such as demarketing), since one may assume only a marginal influence of the recession on the demand

Elasticity of the original supply of the product (or products). An elastic supply curve makes it more possible for the company to include a greater portion of anti-recession measures in its adjustment mix

Competition. Stiffer competition tends to treat the inflation-recession environment relatively more in terms of anti-recession measures, which tends to influence the company to follow suit, so as not to lose its competitive position in the market. This may mean increased demand but lower profitability, since the costs of production and promotion have been going up

Consumer perception, attitude, and expectation. When consumers perceive the situation as basically an inflation and expect it to continue as such, management should utilize more anti-inflation measures in the mix; the contrary is true when consumers perceive the climate as mainly a recession. However, because consumer realities, sentiments, and uncertainties change quite rapidly, management may be required to utilize a very flexible anti-recession, anti-inflation mix.

Nevertheless, quantifying the rate of exchange between anti-inflation and anti-recession measures is extremely difficult. Consequently, one may resort to the construction and evaluation of different anti-inflation-recession packages. For example, one package might include a 10 percent price increase and narrower product line, while another might include a 5 percent price reduction and product downgrading. After such packages are constructed, one may proceed to evaluate their performance according to whatever criteria are chosen by the company (such as profits, competition, company image).

Steel, aluminum, and synthetic fibers are three major industries trying to deal with an inflation-recession environment.

In the last three years, for example, the steel industry has been operating under conditions of (1) very weak demand because the major consumers of steel—the automobile industry, and the appliances and housing industries—decreased their demand as they faced demand reduction for their own products, and (2) rising costs: about 30% increase in the cost of producing sheet and strip, but only 12% increase of their price (Wall Street Journal 1976).

Although the market was very weak, the steel industry increased its list prices 6% in September, 1976. However, because of the weak market and strong competition many companies were willing to sell at the old price. Thus, the attempt to make an anti-inflation adjustment in a market which was experiencing recessionary pressures as well, failed because the recessionary pressures appeared to be stronger than the inflationary pressures (New York Times 1976b).

However, as production costs have nevertheless been going up, and in spite of the weak market, the steel companies declared another price increase of 6% in

December, 1976. This time the price increase held
up. Then, apparently experiencing or perceiving
stronger inflationary pressures than recessionary
pressures, major steel companies once more increased their list price of various items (6% or more)
in May of 1977, and once again in July, 1977. To
some extent, these price increases held up due to government protection against Japanese import or dump-
ing. With such a protection and increasing inflationary pressures steel prices rose 8.7% from July, 1977
to July, 1978, and another increase in list price of
3.2% in January, 1979 (Wall Street Journal 1977).

Similarly, Reynolds has increased the price of aluminum (6%) and Du Pont increased the price of man-
made fibers (10%). Whether these price increases
will materialize or not, depends on the relative impact of the inflation-recession mix on these industries (New York Times 1976b).

Consistent with the above examples is a relatively new hypothesis suggesting that inflation and recession are not separate,
independent, or mutually exclusive forces but, rather, reinforce
each other, at least within a certain range. Existing data seem to
suggest that in some countries (Britain, Canada, and Italy are good
examples) rising inflation and rising unemployment (which indicate
a climate of recession) are mutually reinforcing. If this holds true
on the industry and company level, it might suggest that the task of
adjusting to the inflation-recession climate becomes relatively
easier because as one fights inflation, at least some recessionary
pressures are automatically taken care of (Friedman 1977).

Recession-Shortage

Recession calls for a strategy to stimulate faltering demand,
while shortage calls for a demarketing strategy aimed at achieving
a contrary goal: demand reduction in the short run and demand adjustment in the long run. Thus, the two principal strategies called
for are quite contradictory, as are the tactics utilized to carry
them out. As one can see from Table 2.1, the tactics of price,
promotion, distribution, and consumer selection in climates of recession and shortage are opposite. While recession calls for price
cuts or price-structure change, looser credit, more promotion,
wider distribution, and the cultivation of even marginally profitable

accounts and territories, a shortage climate calls for price increases, tighter credit, less (and different) promotion, limited
distribution, and dropping marginally profitable accounts and territories. Only product tactics are similar, in that basically both climates suggest the offering of cheaper, more functional products.
But even this similarity stems from different reasons: low purchasing power in a recession climate, and high prices for scarce products in a climate of shortages.

In a situation similar to the inflation-recession climate, the
economy, industry, and company may each be confronted with a different impact mix of recession and shortage climates. Additionally,
the company may be viewed as confronted with a specific trade-off
matrix having a variable rate of exchange between anti-recession
and anti-shortage measures.

One can change the axis of anti-inflation measures in Figure
2.1 to anti-shortage measures and principally follow the analysis
advanced in the previous section. That is, one can show that as the
company utilizes more measures to cope with the impact of one climate (such as shortage), it becomes less able to defend itself
against the negative impact of the other climate (such as recession).
The optimal mix—actually the least of the evils—of anti-recession
and anti-shortage measures is influenced by such variables as the
following:

The relative impact of shortages and recession on the company.
   The company should treat its economic environment as mainly a
   shortage environment when the impact of shortages is stronger
   than that of recession, and it should take anti-recession steps
   when the impact of recession is stronger than that of the shortages.
The elasticity of the demand curve. A relatively inelastic demand
   curve enables the company to treat the shortage-recession combination as relatively more of a shortage, and the contrary when
   the demand is elastic. This is because price increases in the
   first situation will have little negative effect on demand, while in
   the second situation the company may be required to cut cost (or
   not raise prices) in order to strengthen the weakening demand.
The elasticity of the supply curve. A relatively elastic supply curve
   enables the company to include more anti-recession measures in
   its adjustment mix, while a relatively inelastic supply curve
   forces the company to include more anti-shortage measures.
   This is because a relatively elastic curve implies lower marginal
   cost than a relatively inelastic supply curve.
Competition. Stiffer competition tends to make a company treat
   the recession-shortage environment relatively more in terms

of anti-recession measures. This may bring about a fuller but less profitable demand.

Consumer perception and expectation. The company's adjustment mix of anti-shortage and anti-recession measures must correlate positively with consumer perceptions and expectations. A gap between consumer expectations and the company's adjustment behavior implies that a nonoptimal mix of anti-shortage, anti-recession measures is at work.

A case in point is that of Burlington, one of the leaders in the textile industry:

> About two-third of Burlington's sales is in yarns and fabrics for various apparel markets. The remaining third . . . come from home furnishings, particularly carpets and draperies. In 1974 the company experienced serious shortages of workers, energy, and fibers. Later it also experienced the impact of recessionary pressures. Burlington response . . . included: (1) product pruning: blankets were eliminated, the output of upholstery fabrics was trimmed, and a vinyl fabric venture was sold; (2) trying to get as many products as possible to their finished state as a means to improve profitability; and (3) reshuffling of top management (BusinessWeek 1974b).

Inflation-Recession-Shortage

An economic climate characterized by simultaneous pressure of inflation, recession, and shortage (IRS) is experiencing the most contradictory pressures of all economic environments: increasing costs and faltering demand; rising prices and increasing unemployment; shortages and excess capacity. In short, it is an environment of multiple paradoxes, uncertainties, and rapid changes. Consequently the impact of IRS on the national economy at the industry level cannot be generalized to the company level. Rather, the company must determine the effects of IRS on its performance and take steps to cope with the situation.

A product-by-product analysis may be required. As shown in Figure 2.2, the company is confronted by a three-way trade-off matrix with a variable rate of exchange among anti-inflation, anti-recession, and anti-shortage measures. Point A, for example, represents respective measures of anti-recession, anti-inflation, and anti-shortage of b, c, and d. This represents an extremely complex situation, in that any measure taken by the company (such as an anti-recession measure) may increase the negative impact of the company's other environments (such as inflation and shortage). Necessarily, the optimal mix among the three types of measures is one representing a minimax solution—a solution minimizing the negative effects of the economic environment. This optimal mix is influenced by the same variables that influence all other types of stagflation: the relative impact of each of the three climates, the elasticity of the demand curve, the elasticity of the supply curve, the nature of the competition, and the consumers' sentiments, attitudes, and expectations.

FIGURE 2.2

The Trade-off Matrix among Anti-Recession,
Anti-Inflation, and Anti-Shortage Measures

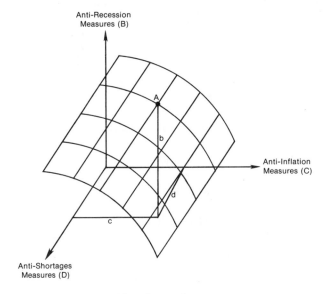

Source: Constructed by the author.

Again, because quantification of the trade-off among the various adaptive measures is virtually impossible, the construction and evaluation of different marketing-mix adjustment packages may be an alternative. Also, the result may be that a company will adopt different adjustment mixes for different products or product lines. For example:

A case in point is General Mills. To understand how consumers are reacting to their total life situation, it hired Yankelovich, Skelly, and White to conduct large-scale consumer studies. The result, among other things, was Breakfast Squares—a new instant breakfast commanding 30% of the market.

To control costs more effectively, cost projection is made for each operating division. Every 90 days actual and anticipated costs are compared, and corrections for the year ahead are made. General Mills also makes full use of contingency planning which enables it to deal effectively with the rapidly changing market.

The net result is a somewhat more careful, conservative company whose profit margin is better than the industry's average (BusinessWeek 1976a).*

Another case in point is Rohr Industries, Inc.

Up to 1975 Rohr drew all its sales from aerospace. However, because of (1) shortages of basic raw materials such as aluminum, nickel, and copper, (2) soaring cost of energy, (3) weak demand, and (4) an overall slow moving economy, Rohr decided to adjust its marketing mix. As a result, Rohr has been shifting its market mix toward energy-conserving transportation systems such as mass transit (BusinessWeek 1975c).†

While the theoretical distinctions among the various types of stagflation are fairly clear, sensitive operational measures facilitating such distinctions in reality are yet to be devised. This is because manifestation of one type of economic climate (such as shortage) can often be interpreted as a manifestation of another (such as inflation); and, more important, because of economic interdependencies, a manifestation of one type of economic climate (such as

_____

*Reprinted from the March 8, 1976, issue of BusinessWeek by special permission, © 1976 by McGraw-Hill, Inc., New York, N.Y. 10020. All rights reserved.

†Reprinted from the April 14, 1975, issue of BusinessWeek by special permission, © 1975 by McGraw-Hill, Inc., New York, N.Y. 10020. All rights reserved.

recession) may actually have been triggered by another climate
(such as shortage).

In the remainder of this chapter, stagflation is conceived of
as any combination of inflation, recession, and shortage.

THE EFFECTS OF STAGFLATION

To obtain a more systematic and quantitative knowledge about
the effects of stagflation, the author sent out a survey questionnaire
designed to measure the effects of stagflation on marketing management and the subsequent changes in strategies and tactics. The
population frame used in the study was Fortune 500 companies. Of
the systematic sample drawn from the Fortune 500 cluster, 104
companies responded. All questionnaires were addressed to the
vice-president of marketing, all items were Likert-type five-point
scales. Items made statements concerning the effects of the economic environment on the components of the marketing mix, or concerning the different adjustment measures. Respondents were asked
to indicate the degree to which such effects and adjustments were experienced by their company (the scale points were "very much,"
"much," "somewhat," "little," and "not at all").

The Impact on Marketing-Mix Decisions

Stagflation has drastically influenced marketing management.
As can be seen from Table 2.2, all marketing-management decisions concerning target consumers, product, price, promotion, and
place were drastically affected. Yet, Table 2.2 also shows that not
all the decision areas were affected equally. Thus, as far as the
"very much" and "much" columns indicating drastic effects, the
rank order of such effects on the various decision areas was price,
product, consumers, promotion, and place.

Price

Stagflation has drastically affected the pricing policy decisions
of 86 out of the 104 responding companies (82.7 percent of the
sample). Only two companies were not affected at all. In addition,
consumer credit decisions of 39 companies (37.5 percent of the
sample) were drastically affected. The possible reasons for such
extreme effects on price decisions are that the very nature of stagflation expresses itself in dollars and cents, and that the influence
of stagflation on price decisions is more immediate, while its influence on the other elements of the marketing mix takes more time to
emerge.

TABLE 2.2

Degrees of Stagflation Effects on Marketing Management Decisions

Decision Area Affected	Very Much		Much		Somewhat		Little		No Effect		No Response		Total	
	No.	%	No.	%	No.	%	No.	%	No.	%	No.	%	No.	%*
Price														
Pricing policy	38	36.5	48	46.2	12	11.5	4	3.8	2	1.9	—	—	104	100.0
Consumer credit	13	12.5	26	25.0	25	24.0	21	20.2	11	10.6	8	7.7	104	100.0
Product														
Product line	11	10.6	24	23.1	33	31.7	23	22.1	13	12.5	—	—	104	100.0
Product elimination	15	14.4	19	18.3	38	36.5	19	18.3	13	12.5	—	—	104	100.0
Research and development	6	5.8	20	19.2	25	24.0	36	34.6	16	15.4	1	1.0	104	100.0
Consumers														
Consumer selection	7	6.7	20	19.2	34	32.7	25	24.0	14	13.5	4	3.8	104	100.0
Consumer services	7	6.7	11	10.6	25	24.0	33	31.7	21	20.2	7	6.7	104	100.0
Promotion														
Promotion budget	8	7.7	23	22.1	42	40.4	24	23.1	6	5.8	1	1.0	104	100.0
Media selection	5	4.8	15	14.4	38	36.5	27	26.0	18	17.3	1	1.0	104	100.0
Promotion appeal	4	3.8	14	13.5	39	37.5	29	27.9	15	14.4	3	2.9	104	100.0
Personal selling	5	4.8	18	17.3	41	39.4	28	26.9	12	11.5	—	—	104	100.0
Public relations	3	2.9	18	17.3	30	28.8	31	29.8	22	21.3	—	—	104	100.0
Place														
Channels of distribution	4	3.8	8	7.7	21	20.2	37	35.6	34	32.7	—	—	104	100.0

*Percentages are rounded.
Source: Compiled by the author.

Product

The effects on the product line, product elimination, and research and development were strong, but not extreme. Only about one-third of the companies stated that product line and product elimination were "much" or "very much" affected, and about one-third stated "little" or "no" effect.

Consumers

Marketing management's decisions concerning consumer selection and consumer services were moderately affected. Consumer-selection decisions of only 27 companies (25.9 percent) were affected "much" or "very much," while consumer-service decisions of only 18 companies (17.3 percent) were so affected. (Note the relatively high rate of "No Response" for consumer decisions.)

Promotion

The influence of stagflation on decisions concerning promotion budget, media selection, personal selling, and public relations was very moderate. Of all five promotion areas, promotion budget decisions were most influenced: 31 companies (29.8 percent) were "much" or "very much" affected, and 30 companies stated little or no effect. Least affected were decisions dealing with public relations. It should be noted that over 40 percent of the companies reported little or no effects of stagflation on media selection, and promotion appeal. The implication of this finding is that a considerable portion of the Fortune companies surveyed did not detect changes in their consumers and the economic environment to call for changes in these decision areas.

Place

Channels-of-distribution decisions were only moderately affected by stagflation. Channel decisions of 12 out of the 104 companies surveyed (11.5 percent) were drastically affected, while 71 companies (68.3 percent) stated little or no effect.

Adjustments to Stagflation

Table 2.3 presents adjustment measures and the degree to which they were adopted by the sample. As can be seen, most drastic adjustments were made in the area of pricing and the least drastic in the areas of promotion and place. This is congruent with the findings reported in Table 2.2 concerning the effects of the perceived

TABLE 2.3

Adjusting Marketing Mix to Stagflation

Marketing Mix	Degree of Adjustment												
	Very Much		Much		Somewhat		Little		None		No Response		Total	
	No.	%	No.	%	No.	%	No.	%	No.	%	No.	%	No.	%*
Price														
Frequent price adjustments	31	30.8	40	38.5	20	19.2	10	9.6	2	1.9	—	—	104	100.0
Stronger emphasis on profit margin	27	26.0	38	36.5	20	19.2	11	10.6	6	5.8	2	1.9	104	100.0
Competitive pricing	8	7.7	30	28.8	27	26.0	28	26.9	8	7.7	3	2.9	104	100.0
Stricter credit	12	11.5	49	47.1	27	26.0	13	12.5	3	2.9	—	—	104	100.0
Extra services to justify higher prices	2	1.9	8	7.7	32	30.8	38	36.5	22	21.2	2	1.9	104	100.0
Consumers														
Avoiding marginal accounts	11	10.6	46	44.2	25	24.0	14	13.5	7	6.7	1	1.0	104	100.0
Better servicing of faithful accounts	13	12.5	39	37.5	29	27.9	10	9.6	11	10.6	2	1.9	104	100.0
Consumer research	6	5.8	19	18.3	18	17.3	26	25.0	34	32.7	1	1.0	104	100.0
Carrying even marginally profitable products to satisfy consumers	4	3.8	18	17.3	29	27.9	34	32.7	16	15.4	3	2.9	104	100.0
Capitalizing on new markets	3	2.9	9	8.7	32	30.8	29	27.9	29	27.9	2	1.9	104	100.0

Product													
Product line reduction	14	13.5	26	25.0	39	37.5	16	15.4	9	8.7	—	—	104	100.0
Increased research and development	7	6.7	33	31.7	28	26.9	25	24.0	11	10.6	—	—	104	100.0
Developing alternative raw materials	10	9.6	26	25.0	30	28.8	28	26.9	9	8.7	1	1.0	104	100.0
Promotion													
Discounting slow-moving products	22	21.2	31	29.8	29	27.9	17	16.3	5	4.8	—	—	104	100.0
Increasing use of coupons	16	15.4	34	32.7	23	22.1	18	17.3	12	11.5	1	1.0	104	100.0
Increasing promotion budget	5	4.8	12	11.5	33	31.7	29	27.9	25	24.0	—	—	104	100.0
Broadening sales force responsibilities	1	1.0	16	15.4	50	48.1	24	23.1	13	12.5	—	—	104	100.0
Place													
Reexamining distribution channels	8	7.7	36	34.6	25	24.0	17	16.3	16	15.4	2	1.9	104	100.0
Receptiveness to selling wholesale to consumers	1	1.0	5	4.8	12	11.5	18	17.3	66	63.5	2	1.9	104	100.0

*Percentages are rounded.

Source: Compiled by the author.

degree of stagflation on the marketing mix. In addition, within each component of the marketing mix, different degrees of adjustment measures were adopted. For example, while 30.8 percent of the companies surveyed shifted (very much so) to frequent price adjustments, only 11.5 percent changed to stricter credit policies.

More specifically, adjustments made in the marketing mix (assuming that "very much" and "much" designate drastic adjustments) are shown below.

Price

The most pronounced adjustments in the price mix were frequent price adjustments (69.3 percent) and greater emphasis on profit margin (62.5 percent). These two adjustments are related in that frequent price adjustments are made primarily to obtain a target profit margin. Such a margin is often widened in anticipation of increased inflationary pressures and shrinking total profits.

Additionally, 36.5 percent of the responding companies emphasized a more competitive pricing strategy and 58.6 percent enacted stricter credit policies, but very few added extra services to justify higher prices.

On the basis of these findings, one can infer that the emerging direction in pricing policy resulting from stagflation is one aimed at three related goals: profitability, which is explained by the frequent price adjustments and the increased emphasis on profit margin; competitive pricing; and stricter credit policy, so that prices can be kept as low as possible.

Consumers

The majority of the companies changed their consumer policies by avoiding marginal accounts in order to keep costs down (54.8 percent), and by preferential treatment of faithful accounts (50.0 percent). Fewer companies (24.1 percent) increased consumer research—presumably to find out how consumers were adjusting to the new environment—so that an improved, possibly more profitable, marketing mix could be offered to them. Only 12 companies strongly capitalized on new markets created by stagflation.

To build or keep customer goodwill, 21.1 percent of the sample continued to carry products that became only marginally profitable as a result of stagflation.

Product

The product-mix decisions were adjusted by about 40 percent of the companies. Thus, product-line pruning, increased research and development, and developing alternative raw materials were taken as complementary product-mix changes.

Promotion

While only 16.3 percent of the respondents increased their promotion budget, and a similar percentage broadened sales force responsibilities, 51.0 percent discounted slow-moving products and 48.1 percent increased the use of coupons as a promotional tool. Thus, it seems that the main adjustments made in response to stag-flation represent changes in the promotion mix more than changes in the promotion budget.

Place

While many companies (42.3 percent) reexamined the channels of distribution, only a few (5.8 percent) became more receptive to the idea and practice of selling to final consumers at wholesale out-lets.

Perhaps such slow adjustments not only stimulated the increase of legitimate cut-rate stores, but also motivated the rapid develop-ment of the independent street vendors (ISV) in major metropolitan areas. While there are few statistics about the ISV, their increased presence in large cities is unmistakable (Sheppard 1979). In New York City, for example, ISV are doing business even in front of Bloomingdales's, Tiffany's, and Saks Fifth Avenue (Dullea 1978). In addition, the ISV are upgrading their product lines and consumer services. Clothing by top designers such as Yves Saint Laurent and Christian Dior are offered to customers, who may pay by per-sonal check, and may even place orders for future delivery (Shama et al. 1979).

Implications

As will be demonstrated in Chapter 4, stagflation has changed consumer behavior drastically. As a result, rules of thumb that many corporations may have developed concerning their target groups may have become less accurate. Decisions based on such outdated rules of thumb may be very costly. Consequently, consumer research becomes more imperative than ever. Yet only 24.1 percent of the companies surveyed had increased their consumer research efforts. Such research may result in redefinition of the target group or groups; different degrees of product and product-line modification resulting from the fact that benefits derived from product features or components may have changed because of stagflation; and changes in distribution, promotion budget, and advertising appeal.

More specifically, the following recommendations to marketing management can be made on the basis of the findings in Tables 2.2 and 2.3:

Price:
1. Keep all costs down, so that price rises may be kept at a minimum. This can be achieved through controlling or even reducing major costs, usually labor and materials; by increasing productivity; by hiring part-timers; by changing fixed costs to variable costs; by standardizing; by buying some parts rather than manufacturing them; and by product-by-product profit analysis
2. Adjust prices frequently, so as to maintain a desired profit margin
3. Change price differentials among products in the line to influence total demand
4. Centralize price decisions so that price changes can be made most efficiently
5. Monitor consumer credit policy, and the credit market for the purpose of borrowing

Products:
1. Shorten product line
2. Offer cheaper, more functional products
3. Purchase raw materials more carefully and strategically
4. Use less-expensive or lower-grade materials in production
5. Introduce substitute products
6. Increase productivity, and innovate

Promotion:
1. Reexamine the size and distribution of promotion budget
2. Change promotional appeals in order to reach target consumers more effectively

Place:
1. Increase or limit distribution to make products more or less available, so as to influence total demand
2. Consider offering at least some products directly to the consumers so as to increase total demand

Consumers: In addition to consumer research, consider the following:
1. Selective treatment of consumers so as to maximize consumer loyalty
2. Drop marginal accounts when possible

SUMMARY AND CONCLUSIONS

Marketing management will continue to operate under conditions of stagflation. A taxonomy of the various types of stagflation has been presented and discussed in this chapter. Stagflation includes inflation-shortage, inflation-recession, recession-shortage, and inflation-recession-shortage. Unlike the basic economic forces (inflation, recession, and shortage), stagflation environments are complex and contain many contradicting pressures. Consequently managerial action taken in response to stagflation is not easily reached, nor is it always effective. Table 2.1, as well as the trade-off analysis and its variables, offer marketing management a conceptual and systematic framework with which to begin.

Quantitatively, the survey results reported in Tables 2.2 and 2.3 indicate that the greatest impact of stagflation on marketing management was in the area of cost or price, followed by product, promotion, and channels. Marketing-mix adjustments were relative to the degree of impact.

Equally important is the fact that the various types of stagflation represent progressive states of complexity, uncertainty, and sluggishness affecting the company at large. As a result accurate predictions become rare. The company is confronted with unexpected situations, making a quick and effective response—when most needed—almost impossible. In addition, when change brought about by marketing-mix adjustments does take place, it occurs slowly because of the many offsetting elements of stagflation. These slow rates of change may affect the company in many ways: past investments made on the basis of return on investment or net expected value may actually result in losses; as a result investors may prefer other, more attractive opportunities; marketing management experienced in dealing with customary high rates of growth may not only be unable to deal with low rates of change, but may also look for other environments—such as foreign markets—that provide the familiar fast-moving economy. That is, the company may not have the human resources to deal with the above economic climates. Above all, the company may not have the capacity to comprehend the effects of economic conditions on its performance, and thus may be unable to modify its policies to minimize possible negative effects and take advantage of opportunities that such conditions may pose (La Placa and Tucker 1976; Hempel and La Placa 1975).

Clearly, more stagflation research is needed. Complementary avenues for such research are developing clear and acceptable criteria to determine, and differentiate among, inflation, recession, and shortage; studies designed to quantify the trade-offs among the components of the types of stagflation; and specific case histories

of industries and companies that analyze how various types of stagflation were handled.

Although stagflation was analyzed mainly from marketing management's point of view, its broader implications to other business
functions are important as well. Even more basic, and thus more
far-reaching, are the consumer behavior and societal manifestations of stagflation, which are discussed in detail in the following
chapters.

REFERENCES

Barmash, Isadore. 1976. "Nationwide Survey Finds Retailers Lack
    Array of Merchandise Formerly Offered." New York Times,
    March 3.

Beauregard, Raymond R., and James A. Pilling. 1974. "The
    Energy Crisis and Its Implications for Marketers." Marketing
    News, January 15, p. 3.

Beizer. 1973. "Shortage Material Expand Inventories and Frighten
    Buyers." Iron Age, December 6, pp. 48-49.

Bennet, K. W. 1973. "Material Pinch Puts the Squeeze on Profits."
    Iron Age, May 17, pp. 37-38.

Braun, A. R. 1976. "Inflation and Stagflation in the International
    Economy." Finance and Development 3 (Spring): 29-32.

BusinessWeek. 1974a. "The Squeeze on the Product Mix." Janu-
    ary 5, pp. 50-55.

_____. 1974b. "Giant Burlington Faces Trying Times for Textile."
    March 2, pp. 44-51.

_____. 1974c. "Pricing Strategy in an Inflation Economy." April
    6, pp. 42-46.

_____. 1974d. "Olin Slims Down for Faster Growth." August 10,
    pp. 60-68.

_____. 1974e. "How to Fight Inflation and Recession." December
    4, pp. 84-88.

_____. 1975a. "The Recession Catches up with Credit Cards."
    February 17, p. 47.

_____. 1975b. "The Retail Push to Keep Inventories Down." March 31, pp. 62-64.

_____. 1975c. "Marketing When Growth Slows." April 14, pp. 44-50.

_____. 1976a. "The Hard Road of Food Processors." March 8, pp. 50-54.

_____. 1976b. "The Silent Crisis in R&D." March 8, pp. 90-92.

_____. 1977. "Coffee Tries to Regain Its Lost Customers." December 26, pp. 33-34.

Cappo, J. 1973. "Will Marketing Run out of Energy?" Chicago Daily News, November 27, p. 34.

Craven, D. 1974. "Marketing Management in an Era of Shortages." Business Horizons 17 (February): 79-85.

Cullwick, D. 1975. "Positioning Demarketing Strategy." Journal of Marketing 39 (April): 51-57.

Dullea, G. 1978. "Those Upwardly Mobile Street Peddlers." New York Times, December 11, p. D13.

Fiedler, E. R. 1975a. "Economic Policies to Control Stagflation." Proceedings of the Academy of Political Science 31, no. 4: 169-75.

_____. 1975b. "Threats to Recovery." Conference Board Record 12, no. 12: 2-5.

Forbes. 1975. "FIFO to LIFO." March 1, pp. 44-45.

Friedman, M. 1977. "Nobel Lecture: Inflation and Unemployment." Journal of Political Economy 85: 451-72.

Fuss, N. H., Jr. 1975. "How to Raise Prices—Judiciously—to Meet Today's Conditions." Harvard Business Review 53 (May).

Griffiths, B. 1976. Inflation: The Price of Prosperity. New York: Holmes and Meier.

Hanna, N., A. H. Kizinbash, and A. Smart. 1975. "Marketing Strategy under Conditions of Economic Scarcity." Journal of Marketing 39 (January): 63-80.

Hempel, D. J., and P. J. LaPlaca. 1975. "Strategic Planning in a Period of Transition." Industrial Marketing Management 4: 305-14.

Kelley, E. J., and L. R. Scheewe. 1975. "Buyer Behavior in a Stagflation/Shortages Economy." Journal of Marketing 39 (April): 44-50.

Kotler, P. 1973. "The Major Tasks of Marketing Management." Journal of Marketing 37 (October): 42-49.

_____. 1974. "Marketing During Periods of Shortage." Journal of Marketing 38 (July): 20-29.

Kotler, Philip, and V. Balachandran. 1975. "Strategic Remarketing: The Preferred Response to Shortages and Inflation." Sloan Management Review (Fall).

La Placa, P. J., and L. R. Tucker, Jr., eds. 1976. Strategic Planning in a Period of Transition. Storrs: University of Connecticut.

Lerner, A. P. 1977a. "Stagflation—Its Causes and Cure." Challenge 20 (September-October): 14-19.

_____. 1977b. "From Pre-Keynes to Post-Keynes." Social Research 44: 387-415.

Mercz, C. M. 1975. "Inflation and Cost Control." Administrative Management 36, no. 1 (January): 20-21.

Monroe, K., and A. Zoltners. 1977. "Pricing During Periods of Scarcity." Working Paper, Polytechnic Institute, State University of Virginia.

Nekvasil, C. A. 1974. "Marketing in Time of Shortages." Industry Week 18 (March 18): 23-28.

Neuman, J. L. 1975. "Make Overhead Cuts That Last." Harvard Business Review 53 (May).

New York Times. 1976a. " Angry Steel Buyers Say Prices Are
Going up in a Weak Market and Du Pont Increases Fiber Prices."
December 1, p. 1.

_____. 1976b. "Du Pont Increasing Fiber Prices; Aluminum In-
flated by Reynolds Also." December 1, p. 1.

Okun, M. A. 1977. "The Great Stagflation Swamp." Brookings Staff
Papers on Economic Activity. Washington, D.C.: Brookings Institution.

Rothe, J. , et al. 1977. "New Product Development under Conditions
of Scarcity and Inflation." University of Michigan Business Review 29 (May): 16-22.

Schendel, D. E. , and G. R. Patton. 1976. "Corporate Stagnation
and Turnaround." Journal of Economics and Business 28 (Spring-
Summer): 236-41.

Shama, A. 1978. "Management and Consumers in an Era of Stagflation." Journal of Marketing 42 (July): 43-52.

Shama, A. 1979. "Off the Wall Selling." Working paper, Graduate School of Business, Baruch College.

Sheppard, N. 1979. "Street Peddlers Proliferating in U.S. Cities."
New York Times, September 4, p. A14.

Sherman, H. 1977. "Monopoly Power and Stagflation." Journal of
Economic Issues 11, no. 2 (June): 269-84.

Silk, L. 1976. "Dr. Burns's Cures vs. Keynesian Medicine." New
York Times, November 18, p. 69.

Stidger, C. H. , and R. W. Stidger. 1976. Inflation Management.
New York: Wiley and Sons.

Wall Street Journal. 1976. "Some Steel Customers See Level Demand for Flat-Rolled over Near Terms." December 2, p. 4.

_____. 1977. "U.S. Steel Undercuts Price Boosts Announced by
Republic and Lykes." May 10, p. 3.

Weiss, E. B. 1974. "Here Are 29 Checkpoints for Marketing Planning in an Era of Shortages." Advertising Age 49 (April 15): 37-38.

3
STAGFLATION AND
SOCIAL REVOLT

The impact of stagflation on people in their roles as consumers, employees, family members, and individuals will be discussed at great length in Chapter 4. In doing so, it will be shown that stagflation has influenced most people negatively; that those who were affected more negatively changed their attitudes and behavior more drastically in both 1976 and 1978; that those who perceived themselves as affected negatively by stagflation tended to belong to the middle class: professionals, managers, middle-income individuals, and college graduates; and that the relationships between the impact of, and adjustments to, stagflation is curvilinear: small increases in the perceived impact of stagflation are associated with drastic and wide-scope behavioral and attitudinal adjustments.

The main goal in this chapter is to focus more clearly on the impact of stagflation on the middle class by examining research findings and reports. While the concepts of "middle class" and "lower class" are used here for purposes of convenience, the marketing, social, and political implications may be totally different, depending on whether middle-income, college-graduate, white-collar workers perceive themselves to be more or less negatively influenced by stagflation than do low-income, less-educated, blue-collar workers.

Portions of this chapter are adapted from Avraham Shama, "Thomas Hobbes, Meet Howard Jarvis: The Impact of Stagflation on Society," Public Opinion 1, no. 5 (November-December 1978): 56-59, published by the American Enterprise Institute.

IMPACT AND SOCIAL CLASS

On the basis of limited but growing empirical research and much intuition, specialists in the field seem to agree that most Americans are negatively affected by stagflation (see, for example, Ackley 1978; Feldstein 1978; Kelley and Scheewe 1975; Linden 1977; Shipchandler 1976; Time 1978). This proposition is also strongly supported in Chapter 4. However, when the question focuses on which groups feel the stagflation crunch most negatively, opinions vary significantly.

There are those who argue that the poor or lower socioeconomic classes suffer from stagflation more than any other groups do. Proponents of this thesis, which may be called the "lower-class thesis," seem to treat stagflation and inflation interchangeably, and report findings consistent with inflation theory.

On the other hand, there are those who argue that, unlike previous economic forces both in form and degree, stagflation seems to affect the middle class more negatively. Prior to the study reported here, this "middle-class thesis" was based mostly on observations of social trends and actions such as survey data and the tax revolt.

The Lower-Class Thesis

An example of research supporting the lower-class thesis is a survey conducted by David Caplovitz in 1975 and reported in 1978. Specifically designed to investigate the impact of both recession and inflation on families in New York, Detroit, Atlanta, and San Francisco, the study oversampled the poor and the retired. It measured the impact of inflation-recession both objectively (by income relative to prices) and subjectively (by changes in attitude and perception), and reported that, measured both ways:

Stagflation affects most families negatively. Fifty-nine percent of the respondents (n = 1,955) stated that relative to the past few years, they were worse off at the time of the survey.

Stagflation affects the poor and the retired more negatively than it does other segments of the society. Accordingly, families that were worse off in 1975 included a high proportion of the poor, the retired, blue-collar workers, Spanish-speaking persons, blacks, and families making under $7,000 annually (Caplovitz 1978a; 1978b; 1979).

For more details of Caplovitz's findings, see Table 3.1.

TABLE 3.1

Impact of Inflation, by Selected Variables
(percent)

	Better Off Now	Stayed Even	Little Worse Off	Lot Worse Off	N
Subsample					
Poor	4	16	37	43	318
Blue-collar	14	28	38	21	575
White-collar	26	26	37	12	758
Retired	6	29	41	25	305
Race-ethnicity					
White	19	28	36	17	1,446
Black	8	17	42	44	400
Spanish-speaking	3	14	36	47	87
Oriental	6	61	33	—	18
Income					
Under $7,000	3	17	39	42	389
$7,000-$12,999	8	23	40	29	39
$13,000-$19,999	15	28	43	14	435
$20,000-plus	33	29	30	8	462
Occupation					
Higher white-collar	24	27	36	13	670
Lower white-collar	18	26	37	19	292
Higher blue-collar	13	26	38	23	341
Lower blue-collar	8	23	38	31	653
Education					
Less than high school	7	24	37	32	606
High school graduate	16	27	39	18	671
Some college	22	24	37	17	330
College graduate	25	25	36	14	347

Source: Caplovitz 1978a, Tables 2.4-2.8.

Thus, stagflation seems to affect people in much the manner postulated by the traditional theory of inflation: the poor, the unskilled, and the retired feel the crunch of stagflation most negatively.

The Middle-Class Thesis

Unfortunately, the thesis equating the impact of stagflation with the impact of inflation seems too simplistic for several reasons:

1. Our experience with the present stagflation has proved that basic economic concepts or theories, such as the Keynesian theory and Phillips curve, are inaccurate or at least not applicable (see Chapter 1). One therefore may question the ease of equating the impact of stagflation and the impact of inflation.
2. If the present economic environment is even remotely similar to that of the Great Depression, as some say it is, then one would certainly find it difficult to equate its impact with that of inflation.
3. A close look at the mood of the public, and its spending and borrowing patterns, including the numerous tax revolt initiatives, makes it difficult to treat the impact of stagflation and that of inflation interchangeably.
4. Most important, there is a growing number of reports showing that the middle class is more negatively influenced by stagflation than are the lower classes. Table 3.2, for example, shows how real after-tax income of various occupations changed from 1967 to 1978. The real after-tax income of traditionally middle-class occupations such as civil service worker, accountant, and university professor regressed anywhere from 2.1 percent to 17.5 percent, while that of traditionally lower-class occupations such as plumber, steelworker, and truck driver gained from 4.5 to 32 percent. As some critics have noted, the middle class is becoming a new poverty class, in that its members feel they no longer can afford their present life-styles. As a result middle-class values are going through an accelerated change that affects consumption patterns as well as the social system (BusinessWeek 1975; see also Newsweek 1977; Roberts 1978; Time 1978; U.S. News and World Report 1977).

Relatedly, because of the progressive income tax structure, the middle class has been paying a greater share of its income as taxes because of nominal income gains. For example, while the upper half of the taxpayers (those whose adjusted gross incomes place them in the upper 50 percent) accounted for 89.7 percent of all income taxes in 1970, they accounted for 92.9 percent of all such

TABLE 3.2

Average Earnings, by Occupation: 1967 and 1978

| Occupation | Average Income | | After-Tax Income | | Percent Change in Income After |
	1967	1978	1967	1978	Taxes and Effects on Inflation
Social Security recipient	$1,012	$3,144	$1,012	$3,144	+59.0
Steelworker	7,548	20,923	6,580	16,932	+32.0
Autoworker	7,647	19,971	6,670	16,114	+24.0
Petrochemical worker	8,273	21,085	7,163	17,072	+22.0
Truck driver	7,134	16,805	6,203	13,779	+14.0
U.S. army major	11,616	26,074	10,171	21,856	+10.0
Plumber	11,149	22,360	9,515	18,045	+4.5
Policeman (municipal)	6,482	13,190	5,665	11,164	+0.9
Federal civil servant (Grade 7)	6,734	13,014	6,182	11,824	-2.1
Computer programmer	9,984	19,604	8,429	15,798	-4.1
Engineer (journeyman)	12,420	23,976	10,585	19,141	-7.5
Corporate lawyer (middle level)	17,208	33,552	14,353	25,636	-8.6
Accountant	7,000	12,800	6,105	10,884	-8.8
U.S. senator	30,000	57,000	24,047	42,168	-10.3
Librarian	7,305	11,894	6,359	10,262	-11.1
Welfare recipient (per family)	1,894	3,089	1,894	3,089	-16.5
University professor	17,158	30,353	14,311	23,077	-17.5

Source: Reprinted by permission from Time, The Weekly Newsmagazine: Copyright Time Inc. 1979.

taxes in 1975. On the other hand, the bottom 50 percent accounted for $10.3 percent in 1970 and only for 7.1 percent in 1975 (Tax Foundation computations). This helps to explain the feeling of some members of the middle class that as their nominal income has progressed, their buying power or real income has regressed. Such feelings are supported by a scientific research project that reported that as accrued comprehensive income (which includes income plus assets) goes up, real purchasing power goes down because of taxes and the drop in the market value of interest-bearing securities (Minarik 1979) (see also Table 4.1).

Yet, economically there is little disagreement that because of stagflation the poor and lower-class consumers must buy and consume less. Nevertheless, in recent years poverty in the United States has become a state of the mind as much as a state of the stomach (Strumpel 1976), and it is such psychological manifestations that seem to have more drastic impact on the middle class. To study this point more clearly and expand our knowledge of the sociopolitical character of stagflation, data from the longitudinal study (to be outlined in Chapter 4) will specifically test the middle-class thesis against the lower-class thesis.

Who bears the burden? To study this point, the "overall impact of stagflation" question (positive, negative, or neutral) was cross-tabulated by socioeconomic data such as occupation, income, employment, age, education, and race.

The results of this analysis are presented in Table 3.3. They suggest (and in a statistically significant way) that in both 1976 and 1978 those who were more negatively affected by stagflation included the following:

Professionals, managers, and those who work in the service industries
Families whose combined income exceeds $20,000
Young (the 18-34 age group was most negatively influenced)
The unemployed
Unmarried persons and those with a nonworking spouse
Caucasians
College graduates

Except for unemployment, the above characteristics can hardly be squared with the definition of "poor" or of low socioeconomic status. Rather, they describe the better-educated and better-off segments of society. In fact, when this unexpected profile first emerged in 1976, data were double- and triple-checked, yielding the same findings that support the proposition that the middle class perceives itself as suffering from stagflation relatively more than

TABLE 3.3

Impact of Stagflation, by Socioeconomic Status
(percent)

	1976 (N = 937)		1978 (N = 779)	
	Negative	Positive	Negative	Positive
Occupation				
Blue-collar	63	37	72	28
Clerical	64	36	65	35
Service	75	25	80	20
Sales	69	31	63	37
Professional	85	15	73	27
Managerial	76	24	77	23
Other	53	47	73	27
Family income				
Up to $10,000	65	35	60	40
$10,000-$19,999	67	33	71	29
$20,000-$29,999	80	20	73	27
$30,000 and up	78	22	82	18
Age				
Up to 34	77	23	71	29
35-49	69	31	74	26
50-64	54	46	75	25
65+	44	56	78	22
Employment				
Employed	71	29	72	28
Unemployed	73	27	93	7
Education				
High school or less	58	42	66	34
Some college	72	28	71	29
College graduate and postgraduate	82	18	77	23
Marital status				
Single	81	19	69	31
Married	65	35	75	25
Divorced	68	32	67	33
Widowed	46	54	67	33
Separated	79	21	67	33
Race				
Black	58	42	51	49
Caucasian	74	26	76	24
Oriental	51	49	62	38
Hispanic	70	30	67	33
Other	69	31	57	43

Notes: Respondents who were neutrally affected by stagflation are not included in this table. Analyzed separately, however, they tend to be similar to those affected positively.

"Negative" includes people who reported "strongly negative," "negative," and "somewhat negative" impact of stagflation.

"Positive" includes people who reported "strongly positive," "positive," and "somewhat positive" impact of stagflation.

Source: Compiled by the author.

other social groups. It was not until two years later, when the second survey was being completed in mid-1978, that results from national surveys were beginning to offer convergent validations of the middle-class proposition. Thus, results from surveys by the Gallup (April 1978), New York Times/CBS (June 1978), and Louis Harris (October 1978) polls suggested that the middle class "believes that other people, from the poor on welfare to the rich who enjoy tax advantages, are somehow getting away with something," while its own members "feel stabbed in the back" (Roberts 1978). Consequently, because of such convergent validations it may be concluded that psychologically stagflation influences the middle class more than it does other social classes.

It should be noted here that the concepts "middle class" and "lower class" are used for purposes of convenience. Our aim is not to establish exact boundaries of various classes, but to show the differential impact of stagflation by income, occupation, and education. The danger in such an analysis is that differences may register as being associated with one variable while in reality they are attributed to another. For example, one may find that different income groups are differently affected by stagflation, while in reality it is the occupation variable that is responsible for the impact and the income differences were found simply because income and occupation covary. To test for such covariations, partial correlation analysis was performed, holding constant those variables that might covary with the variable being cross-tabulated with the impact of stagflation. Specifically, when the impact of stagflation was cross-tabulated with education, the variables of income and occupation were held constant, and so forth.

The results of this partial correlation analysis showed that each of the variables of income, education, and occupation is independently and significantly related to the impact of stagflation in the manner indicated earlier in this discussion and depicted in Table 3.2.

Why the Middle Class?

First, it should be clarified that when measurement is made purely in economic terms, such as disposable or real income (that is, "census income"), the poor, the younger members of the labor force, and those on a fixed income score lowest, thus lending support to the lower-class thesis. This is despite social welfare policies that often minimize the private monetary cost of unemployment, which hits the poor hardest (Ackley 1978; Feldstein 1978). Indeed, in terms of monetary measures—sometimes referred to as objective measures by economists—no one would disagree that the lower social or economic classes suffer from stagflation more than other groups do. Members of the lower class are double victims of stagflation: as a group they are the first to experience unemployment, and since they have few assets, inflation hits them just as hard as, if not harder than, other groups.

However, the findings here suggest that it is the middle class that feels most adversely affected by stagflation, as seen in the 1976 and 1978 surveys (Shama 1978).

To explain this contradiction between the lower-class and the middle-class theses, it seems that one should look for a noneconomic explanation. That is, the stagflation phenomenon, defined in economic terms (although not necessarily originating in that sphere), may best be explained in terms of psychological impact on the middle-class values, life-style, and expectations. More specifically, stagflation has affected the values or motivations considered below.

Economic and Social Affluence

Perhaps more than any other group, the middle class has sought affluence and has believed it to be within reach. Better jobs, higher incomes, and better homes have been the adrenaline of the members of the middle class. Some of them have reached such goals, thus heightening the expectations of others.

With the impact of stagflation, more and more people aspiring to affluence are realizing that such goals are becoming less and less realistic. They therefore must change their values and lower their aspirations.

Thus, the idea that "more is better" or "big is better," so highly ingrained among members of the middle class and so strongly reinforced by business practices to stimulate demand, may now have to change to "less is better" or "small is better." Such a swift and total value change can hardly be achieved smoothly. In such a situation psychological frustration and even revolt against those perceived as responsible for the new situations are logical results. Understandably, business and government become easy and not unlogical targets.

The poor, on the other hand, have never really believed that the American dream would become a reality. For them reality has been characterized by daily economic struggle and political alienation.

Conspicuous Consumption

Associated with affluence is the value of conspicuous consumption, strongly reinforced and capitalized upon by the business sector. As a result of stagflation, the middle class can no longer achieve conspicuous consumption with its diminishing means. Slowly the

conspicuous consumption value is changing to "conspicuous conservation" and to "a new functionalism"—changes brought about by values
of opinion leaders or by lack of any other economic alternative.

Locus of Control

The importance of "being in control," a strong middle- and
upper-class value, has been challenged because of stagflation.
Members of the middle class, perhaps more than any other group,
believed they controlled their lives and were responsible for the
rewards and punishments bestowed upon them. Furthermore, they
also held that they could manipulate their environment to their own
advantage. Planning—whether for buying a house, sending children
to college, or retirement, or as a structured, systematic way of
life—has always been the basis for the future orientation of the
middle class.

Because of the high degree of uncertainty associated with
stagflation, planning by members of the middle class has become
much harder, if not impossible. Relatedly, the feeling of "closure"
or the ability to control one's own life is also lessened, leaving
people shaken and confused.

The poor, on the other hand, have rarely felt in control, so
stagflation does not represent a totally new psychological phenomenon but, rather, a change of degree within existing parameters.
In addition, the poor have indulged less in long-range planning.
Thus, since hand-to-mouth existence has been more characteristic
of the poor, stagflation means less within the existing situation,
rather than a totally new environment.

Social Altruism

Social welfare programs, most of which were designed to help
the poor, have always been highly supported by the middle class,
both politically and financially. Though treating different social
segments differently in order to increase equality has never been
supported so highly as in such welfare states as Great Britain and
Sweden, helping the poor as an altruistic form of behavior is nevertheless a middle-class attribute.

With the impact of stagflation, however, more and more
middle-class members have begun to feel poor, although as measured by the federal government they are far from being so. Nevertheless, many previous supporters of ambitious social programs
have felt that the system is no longer fair to them, and their willing-
ness to pay for such programs directly (through taxation) or indirectly (through federal deficits) has diminished. More egotistic or
selfish values are a logical result that, at least cognitively, will
bother the middle class in the process of adjustment.

IMPLICATIONS

Social

It should be clear that any discussion relating only to the economic or business implications of stagflation may be missing not only important dimensions of this phenomenon but possibly its main essence. Though defined in economic terms, stagflation does not necessarily originate in the economic sphere. As A. H. Hansen pointed out in 1939, a stagnant economy often originates from social stagnation in such areas as innovation and migration. Though innovation and migration may be regarded as economic or business factors, their momentum is certainly determined by expectations (that is, psychological factors). Therefore, the social and political implications of stagflation are at least as important as the economic or business ones, and as such may indicate a drastically different social system.

The most important social implication results from the fact that stagflation indicates slow growth of the national pie—much too slow relative to people's expectations and conditioning. Having gotten used to rapidly improving standards of living, families suddenly face a halt to upward economic and social mobility. Furthermore, as socioeconomic expectations of the post-World War II period materialized, expectations—particularly those of the middle class—increased much further. In this condition, such growing expectations can be satisfied only if increases in real income become more substantial.

Such, however, is not the case during stagflation. The pie, in real terms, grows very slowly. Consequently, the various social groups must compete for a greater share of the pie, which relative to expectations has been shrinking since the mid-1970s. In addition, since middle-class expectations, compared with those of the lower class, are much higher relative to the attainable share of the pie, the result is struggle or militancy to realise at least some aspirations. This militancy is further reinforced by middle-class perceptions of social developments since 1960: monetarily the unskilled, semiskilled, and more blue-collar workers have been joining the middle class—either because of increased income or as a result of social policies. These perceptions help increase the squeeze felt by the middle class, as well as its militancy or "revolt." Yet, some social commentators argue that the real danger for American society lies in the potential revolt of the poor if decision makers shift their focus to the members of the middle class, who can afford "their own houses, doctors, hospitals, recreation, schools, and colleges," and "have secure jobs and incomes. . . . The revolt of the affluent, which now has politicians so frightened, is not a violent thing. The response in the ghettoes if life there is allowed to further deteriorate, might be different" (Galbraith 1979). Perhaps so. But in Chile it was the middle class that revolted because of the impact of inflation (Minard 1978).

The above perceptions and actions sharpen social conflicts and change the course of social development. But, unlike other social phenomena, stagflation brings about a social movement led by and for the middle class. And because the struggle is for limited resources, it is necessarily a struggle against those in control of the resources and those perceived to benefit relatively more from such resources: the lower classes and the allocators—the federal and local governments. Thus, it seems that, unlike the 1960s, in which the struggle was for the poor and the disadvantaged, the struggle of the 1970s was for the "haves" and the relatively advantaged. Hobbesian society seems to have resulted from stagflation, or at least from a growing degree of selfishness. Surely the social character of America has dramatically changed with stagflation.

Political

Following the view that democratic political systems and candidates seek to satisfy their voter-consumers, stagflation is an issue that no candidate or party can resist. Best symbolized by Proposition 13, stagflation appears to be a top issue in all present campaigns and those to come. If one were to judge the success of Proposition 13 and its wide public appeal, proposals to deal with stagflation or the economy effectively—or, better yet, incumbents' evidence of having dealt with it successfully—are viewed as decisive factors in elections. Both major parties are aware of this as they plan for the presidential and other campaigns.

In such environment, incumbents in control of resource allocation, particularly the president, seem to have an advantage. This is because incumbents are in a position to enact policies that can win them votes. It has been shown, for example, that American presidents in the past few decades have enacted monetary and fiscal policies likely to increase voter support (see, for example, Cameron 1978; Tufte 1978). Thus, if correct decisions are made by President Jimmy Carter in 1979 and early 1980, the probability of his winning a second term will increase significantly. President Carter's activities relating to the tax-cut bill—from which, incidentally, middle-income people are said to benefit most—and his tougher stand on inflation indicate that he is aware of this point. The problem, however, is that it is extremely difficult to make correct decisions that enable one to show success in combating both recession and inflation.

Moreover, the findings concerning curvilinear relationships between perceived impact of stagflation and the resulting adjustments, which are reported in Appendix A, reveal an extremely important fact. Accordingly, and unlike the assumption made by economic theories thus far, it was found that any change in people's perception of the overall effect of the "economic situation" is associated with changes in attitudes and behavior as great as a magnitude of three. Consequently, future increases of a few points in the perceived impact of stagflation may make it the only issue of future campaigns, while a similar decrease may make it a nonissue.

Marketing

The finding that middle-class consumers feel more negatively influenced by stagflation than other social classes has important ramifications for marketing management. Since most products, and virtually almost all new products introduced in the mass markets, are targeted at middle-income consumers, it is clear why marketing management should be particularly interested in the impact of stagflation. Furthermore, since consumers with incomes as high as $40,000 think, act, and consume like the middle class, what happens to the middle class is of utmost importance to marketing-mix decisions and business strategy (BusinessWeek 1975).

Figure 3.1 shows how expenditures for various product categories change as a function of household income. Accordingly, "as household earnings increase, expenditures for recreation, the automobile, home furnishing, and apparel expand most rapidly. Outlays for food and shelter, on the other hand, tend to rise more slowly" (Linden 1977). The reverse is also valid: as real income declines, first to be cut are expenditures on products that are sensitive to changes in income: recreation, furniture, and luxuries. Furthermore, within the various product classes in Figure 3.1, including those relatively insensitive to change in income (such as food), the first items to be cut from the family budget are those perceived as luxuries. For example, although expenditures on food are relatively insensitive to changes in income, a decrease in real income is normally associated with reduced purchases of better cuts of meat and prepared food items. In a way stagflation makes the middle class behave more and more like the poor: it must spend a greater share of its income on food because of high food prices (Roger and Green 1978), and thus can afford fewer other products and services. As a result it comes to value the durable, the

FIGURE 3.1

The Classes of Spending

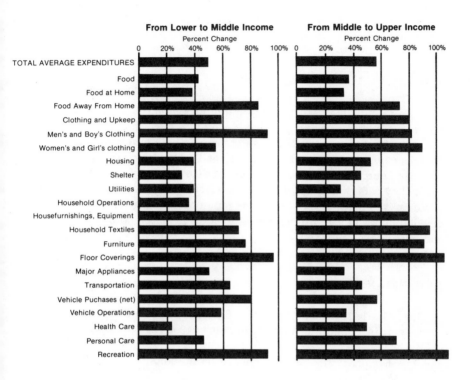

Note: This figure shows the percent increase in spending for selected goods and services as household income increases. For example, as we move from the middle- to the upper-income brackets, total household expenditures for consumption rise by somewhat over 55 percent. Total spending for food, however, grows by about 35 percent, while outlays for recreation more than double. As defined in this presentation, "lower income" includes households in the $5,000-$10,000 earning bracket; "middle income," the $10,000-$20,000 bracket; and "upper income," the $20,000-and-over bracket. All data are based on a survey by the Bureau of Labor Statistics on consumer expenditures in 1973.

Source: Linden 1977, p. 59. © 1977 The Conference Board.

economical, and the functional. Although this is presumably a change in economic decisions resulting from restricted means, it is also a social regression that is perceived as such by the middle class.

Equally important are the resulting changes in middle-class values, which influence subsequent purchase decisions in both the short and the long runs.

SUMMARY

In this chapter the impact of stagflation on the middle class was examined. It was found that the middle class feels more adversely affected by stagflation as compared with other social classes. This has important social, political, and marketing ramifications. Socially, stagflation has brought about a new society that is characterized by a high degree of social conflicts. Politically, stagflation becomes the main issue, if not the only one. The net result of such developments is a totally different system in which both consumers and marketers operate.

REFERENCES

Ackley, G. 1978. "The Cost of Inflation." Proceedings of the American Economic Association 69: 149-54.

BusinessWeek. 1975. "The Squeeze on the Middle Class." March 10, pp. 52-60.

Cameron, D. R. 1978. "Inflation and Fiscal Policy in Eight Nations." A paper delivered at the Annual Meeting of the American Political Science Association, New York, New York.

Caplovitz, D. 1978a. Making Ends Meet: How Families Cope with Inflation and Recession. New York: Institute for Research on Human Affairs, the Graduate Center, City University of New York.

_____. 1978b. "Making Ends Meet: How Families Cope with Inflation and Recession." Public Opinion (May/June): 52-54.

_____. 1979. Making Ends Meet: How Families Cope with Inflation and Recession. Beverly Hills, California: Sage Publications Inc.

Feldstein, M. 1978. "The Private and Social Cost of Unemployment." Proceedings of the American Economic Association 69: 155-58.

Ferretti, F. 1978. "Coping with Inflation: The City and Suburbs." New York Times, June 23, p. B1.

First National City Bank. 1973. "Does Inflation Lean Heaviest on the Poor?" First National City Bank (November).

Galbraith, J. K. 1979. "A Diagnosis of Inflation: Causes and Cures." New York Times, January 12, p. A23.

Green, G. H., and R. O. Nordstrom. 1974. "The Rewards from Being a Disloyal Buyer." Journal of Purchasing 10 (February): 33-40.

Kelley, E., and L. R. Scheewe. 1975. "Buyer Behavior in a Stagflation/Shortages Economy." Journal of Marketing 39, no. 21 (April): 44-50.

Linden, F. 1977. "Downstairs, Upstairs." Across the Board 14, no. 10 (October): 58-61.

Minard, L. 1978. "Chile, Without Tears." Forbes, October 30, pp. 145-48.

Minarik, J. 1979. "Who Wins, Who Loses from Inflation." Challenge 22 (January-February): 26-31.

Newsweek. 1977. "The Middle Class Poor." September 12.

_____. 1978. "The Inflation Surge: Special Report. May 29, pp. 68-82.

Roberts, S. 1978. "Middle Class Thinks Itself Hit Most by Taxes and Inflation." New York Times, August 1, p. 1.

Roger, D., and H. Green. 1978. "Changes in Consumer Food Expenditure Patterns." Journal of Marketing 42, no. 2 (April): 14-19.

Shama, A. 1978. "Thomas Hobbes, Meet Howard Jarvis: The Impact of Stagflation on Society." Public Opinion 1, no. 5 (November-December): 56-59.

Shapiro, J. L., and R. D. Bohmbach. 1978. "The Inflation Worry Hits New Peak." Advertising Age 3 (July 17): 33.

Shipchandler, E. Z. 1976. "Inflation and Life Styles: The Marketing Impact." Business Horizons 19 (February).

Strumpel, B., ed. 1976. Economic Means and Human Needs: Social Indicators of Well-Being and Discontent. Ann Arbor, Mich.: Survey Research Center, Institute for Social Research.

Time. 1978. "Next Round against Inflation." April 24, pp. 66-72.

Tufte, R. E. 1978. Political Control of the Economy. Princeton: Princeton University Press.

U.S. News and World Report. 1977. "The New Breed of Consumers: Growing Challenge to Business." July 25, pp. 45-46.

4

SOCIETY DURING STAGFLATION

INTRODUCTION

According to the traditional economic theory of consumption,
the impact of stagflation on society can be determined by studying
what happens to real purchasing power during stagflation. Real income or real disposable income enables consumers to purchase
various combinations of products and services and to save by post-
poning present consumption. Sometimes, consumers borrow money
in order to increase present consumption. All this is represented
by the "budget constraint line," which theoretically indicates all
combinations of products and services on which the consumer may
spend income. The exact "combination," or "bundle," or "basket,"
however, is determined by the consumer's taste or preferences.

In general, real income declines or stagnates during stagflation, thus forcing consumers to consume less (movement of the
budget constraint line toward the axis) and to change their purchasing habits so as to take advantage of substitutions by buying cheaper
products. For example, in the stagflation years of the 1970s, real
income per consuming unit (families or single persons) declined during four years, and more such declines were expected (Data Resources, Inc. 1978). To minimize the effect of declining income,
many consumers bought cheaper products and services, such as
generic products and no-frills flights. Substitution, however, is not
an unlimited strategy. Therefore it may be concluded that economically the impact of stagflation is to reduce consumption or halt its
growth.

Yet solutions by means of traditional consumption theory are
often insufficient or misleading. Psychologists have often shown
that consumer attitudes and expectations explain purchase behavior

better than income does. The basic conceptualization of the economic studies of the Survey Research Center (SRC), as posed by George Katona, the founder of consumer psychology, is that the consumer's objective environment (income, assets, and opportunities) influences his or her subjective well-being (attitudes and expectations) and determines consumer behavior relating to demand and savings (Katona 1964; see also Katona 1960, 1974, 1975). Katona's basic view of consumers is that they are intelligent and well-informed, and have many useful intuitive rules of thumb that guide their behavior. His studies monitoring cyclical changes in consumer attitudes and behavior have repeatedly supported his view by showing that consumer attitudes are often more important than the objective economic environment.

A striking example of the importance of consumer attitudes in predicting behavior is depicted in Figure 4.1. As can be seen, in the 1970s the consumer confidence index—an attitudinal measure relating to consumer perception of economic conditions—was closely related to buying plans. That is, the consumer's economic outlook and attitudes determine purchasing or spending, regardless of objective reality (income).

In later years Katona's cyclic approach was broadened to include personal goals and aspirations as input variables influencing subjective well-being, and to include social satisfaction/dissatisfaction with prices, employment, and government policies as input variables that determine social-political behavior and exert influence on consumer behavior (see Strumpel 1976a; Morgan 1978; Strumpel 1973, 1974). Although this conceptualization is an accurate depiction of reality, many of the studies based on it are fragmented, in that they consider one facet at a time (such as "the impact of economic reality on values and beliefs") rather than integrated (see Gurin and Gurin 1976; Pfaff 1976; Strumpel 1976b).

The approach taken in Chapter 1 (see Figure 1.2) is similar to the SRC conceptualization. It states that financial resources, attitudes, and expectations determine how consumers behave and cope with stagflation. As a result, both income aspects and attitudinal aspects are discussed in this chapter. However, unlike the SRC projects, the present one is an integrated effort. The longitudinal impact of stagflation on consumers, and the resulting adjustment measures—both economic and attitudinal—are the main focus of the chapter. A comparison of marketing management and consumers during periods of stagflation is a secondary focus.

FIGURE 4.1

Consumer Confidence Index and Buying Plans Index: 1969–78

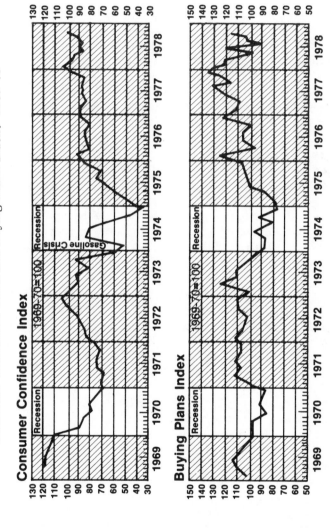

Note: All data are seasonally adjusted.
Source: National Conference Board 1978.

75

ASSESSING THE IMPACT AND ADJUSTMENTS

To assess the general impact of stagflation on society, it is sufficient to show what happens to prices and wages in each type of stagflation:

Inflation-shortage. During inflation-shortage the overall price level goes up, and prices of scarce materials rise even more sharply, while the relative price of labor (wages) goes down. Consumers therefore can no longer expect fast improvements in their standards of living.

Inflation-recession. During inflation-recession there is a net rise in the general price level (inflation), measured by the Consumer Price Index (CPI), although some prices stay steady or decline moderately. Wages exhibit a relative decline.

Recession-shortage. A stagflation of this type indicates that most prices are steady while prices of scarce goods go up. Relative wages decline moderately. Real wages of those who become unemployed due to stagflation fall sharply, resulting in reduced consumption and deteriorating standards of living.

Inflation-recession-shortage. Prices of most products and services go up dramatically, while the relative level of wages declines. The unemployed suffer from both inflation and recession.

Therefore, the general impact of all types of stagflation is that prices of most products and services keep going up while the relative level of wages keeps going down. Table 4.1 presents the consumer price index of all items (CPI) as well as that of food, housing, medical care, and transportation; and a real-income index. As can be seen, CPI has been rising faster than income. Even more alarming is the rise of CPI of the basic necessities—food, housing, medical care, and transportation—which account for a high and growing percentage of consumer spending.

As a result it may be concluded that stagflation is a period during which real and expected consumption can no longer rise as they did in the past. This is because the level of economic growth during stagflation is below potential and because prices of necessities such as housing and medical care rise faster than the overall CPI. Furthermore, because society has been accustomed to high growth rates in real consumption and the standard of living, future growth rates required to produce results that will satisfy consumers must be higher and higher. This, however, is not possible during stagflation. Consequently, besides the economic factors mentioned above, stagflation represents social factors limiting growth (Hirsch 1978).

TABLE 4.1

Income and Consumer Price Indexes, 1970–78

(1967 = 100)

	Real Disposable Income 1970	All Items	Food	Housing	Medical Care	Transportation
1970	n.a.	116.3	114.9	118.9	120.6	112.7
1971	n.a.	121.3	118.4	124.3	128.4	118.6
1972	100.0	125.3	123.5	129.2	132.5	119.9
1973	107.0	133.1	141.4	135.0	137.7	123.8
1974	105.0	147.7	161.7	150.6	150.5	137.7
1975	107.0	161.2	175.4	166.8	168.6	150.6
1976	111.0	170.5	180.7	177.2	184.7	165.5
1977	116.0	181.5	192.6	189.6	202.4	177.2
1978	121.0	195.4	211.4	202.8	219.4	185.5
1979 (Sept.)	124.0	223.4	237.1	234.6	243.7	221.4

Note: Because the base years for income and the CPI are different, only the rates of change relative to each other should be compared.

Sources: U.S. Department of Labor, Bureau of Labor Statistics 1975; 1979; U.S. Department of Health, Education, and Welfare, Social Security Administration, 1976; Bureau of Economics and Statistics 1979.

Theoretically, it is also possible for wage inflation or labor shortage (triggering higher wages) to occur during stagflation. However, when such increases in the price of labor (wages) are higher than increases in other prices, the result is the familiar demand-pull inflation.

Thus, unlike its contradictory pressures on marketing management, stagflation affects society in a more consistent manner: it erodes standards of living and destroys dreams of affluence. As a result, coping strategies for stagflation designed to minimize the negative impact of stagflation include two complementary avenues: consuming less or paying less for products and services, and/or increasing income. Equally important is the psychological impact of stagflation on society, and the resulting changes in attitudes and behavior. More specifically, stagflation affects people in their roles as consumers, employees, family members, voters, and individuals; and in these roles they adjust to it. A summary presentation of possible strategies to cope with stagflation is provided in Table 4.2.

As can be seen in Table 4.2, consumer adjustments to the marketing mix during stagflation may include various coping strategies. In terms of prices consumers may cope by becoming more careful with money, shopping for "specials" and bargains, and using credit more and/or saving less. In terms of products they may cope by buying more private brands and generic products, becoming do-it-yourselfers, and changing the importance given to different product attributes. For instance, functional attributes and durability become more important during stagflation. In terms of place consumers may cope by buying as many products as possible from wholesale or cut-rate outlets. Finally, in terms of promotion they may cope by using as many coupons as possible, while becoming more skeptical about other advertising appeals designed to induce or stimulate demand. Altogether, depending on the depth and impact of stagflation, the result may be a drastically new type of consumer who allocates his or her consumption budget differently, takes less risk, makes more decisions jointly with the spouse, and has different habits and preferences.

Employees may cope by looking for better-paying jobs, working overtime or moonlighting, and sending the spouse or children to work.

Family members may adjust by making more purchase decisions jointly, spending more time together, and even seeking help from social organizations.

As voters and individuals people may cope by changing general and political attitudes, as well as by taking political action, such as the " tax revolt. "

TABLE 4.2

Social Adjustment Strategies for Stagflation

Area	Adjustment Strategy
Consumers	
General	Change allocation of resources
	Change habits and preferences
	Less wastefulness
	Less risk taking
	More joint decisions with spouse
	More rational decision making
	More information gathering before purchase
	Greater importance of functionalism
	More hedging against stagflation
	Seek outside help—social welfare programs
Price	More careful with money
	More comparison shopping
	More shopping for "specials" and bargains
	More use of credit
	Saving less
Product	Consume less
	Purchase cheaper product (private and generic labels)
	Increase importance of durability in durables
	Do-it-yourself
Place	Wholesale shopping
	Shopping at cut-rate stores
Promotion	Use more coupons
Employees	Move to a better-paying job
	Work overtime or moonlight
	Send spouse and/or children to work
	Change attitude toward work
Family members	Change role structure
	Increase joint decision making
	Spend more time together
	Seek outside help
Voters	Change political attitudes
	Initiate change (such as Proposition 13)
Individuals	Change attitudes and values about the American economy and its free-enterprise system

Source: Compiled by the author.

79

Indeed, as will be documented later in this chapter, stagflation affects most people drastically and negatively, and results in extensive use of coping strategies. In addition, although the above coping strategies are interrelated, it is logical to expect that people who are more negatively affected by stagflation will adopt more coping strategies than those less affected. However, some of the most negatively affected people may no longer be able to cope because they have already exhausted all possible measures. For example, a 1975 research project investigating how families have been affected by and have responded to the twin calamities of inflation and recession in four cities reported that the greater the impact of inflation and recession, the more extreme and numerous the adjustment measures taken. At the same time, those experiencing the most negative impact often could do little to cope, and even public assistance did not seem to help much. As a result such people were subject to the greatest mental strain (Caplovitz 1979).

Finally, it should be noted that stagflation has affected some people positively. They may constitute a distinct market segment that is substantial, accessible, and highly profitable.

STUDYING THE IMPACT OVER TIME

Exactly how stagflation affects people is a question that does not lend itself to an easy, conclusive answer. Although from the above discussion, and from general survey data and observations, there seems to be a consensus concerning the drastic impact of stagflation, the extent to which it affects people as consumers, employees, family members, voters, and individuals is yet to be determined. The reason for the lack of such conclusive knowledge lies in the fact that stagflation is a rather new force whose impact is multifaceted. Survey data collected by the Survey Research Center, the Gallup organization, Louis Harris, Inc., the National Opinion Research Center, and various federal agencies, such as the Commerce and Labor departments, were obtained with different questions and economic environments in mind. Although the value of such data is important, they constitute only secondary data with partial answers to questions concerning the impact of stagflation.

To establish the exact impact of stagflation on consumption, family relations, attitudes toward work and employment, and general and political attitudes and behavior, a longitudinal study was designed by the author of this book. It included two interrelated questionnaire surveys that were specifically designed to measure the impact of stagflation and the measures used to cope with it. The surveys were conducted in 1976 and 1978.

The sample utilized in the first survey was drawn from the population of New York City, using age, sex, and race as control variables. Altogether, 969 respondents were interviewed. All questionnaire items were closed-end Likert scales. Scale items were statements concerning the effects of stagflation on consumers or concerning adjustment measures; the respondents were asked to indicate the degree to which they agreed or disagreed with the statement on a seven-point scale. The questionnaire, however, was carefully constructed and pretested to ensure the inclusion of all relevant factors and semantic uniformity. The second survey used essentially the same procedure, sample type, size, and questionnaire (N = 916).

It should be noted that the type of sample utilized in this study (quota, the least convenient of all convenience samples) and sample size were carefully chosen to ensure as much relevance, heterogeneity, and representation as possible, short of full probability samples, which are very costly compared with national probability samples. The respondents in the present longitudinal study tended to be younger and more educated, to have higher family income, and to include more professionals and managers, as well as more nonwhite respondents. A comparison between selected socioeconomic variables of the samples used in the present study and national probability samples appears in Table 4.3. In spite of these socioeconomic differences, perceived social class in our sample and a national probability sample were very similar. In addition, when it was possible to compare the attitudes of our sample with those of national probability samples, the results were often very similar. Nevertheless, the results of the present study can be more easily generalized to consumers in metropolitan areas than to the total population. Most important, however, is the fact that the present study is the only longitudinal study designed to investigate how people are affected by and adjust to stagflation.

Overall Impact

Stagflation drastically influenced consumers in both 1976 and 1978: of the 969 consumers surveyed in 1976, only 3.3 percent stated that stagflation did not have any effect on them; and of the remaining 937, 70.2 percent reported a negative effect. Similarly, of the 916 consumers questioned in 1978, 15.2 percent reported no effect and 74.0 percent of the rest reported a negative effect.

Table 4.4 presents more detailed information on the longitudinal impact of stagflation on consumers. With the realization by over 95 percent of each of the two samples that prices are high,

TABLE 4.3

Comparisons of the Longitudinal Study Samples and National Probability Samples
(percent)

	National Probability Samples		Samples of Longitudinal Study	
	1976	1978	1976	1978
Unemployment[a]	8.5	7.5	8.0	5.6
National	7.7 (1975)	5.8		
Sex[b]				
Male	44.9		49.4	49.9
Female	55.1		50.6	50.1
Race[b]	88.3 (1975)		76.1	76.5
Black	9.7 (1975)		12.7	13.9
Oriental			4.1	3.5
Hispanic			5.8	4.5
Other	2.0 (1975)		1.0	1.5
Education[a]				
Less than high school	35.0	31.0	10.0	7.2
High school graduate	49.0	52.5	52.9	41.6
Some college	1.0	3.0	3.7	5.7
College graduate	10.5	10.0	25.2	30.0
Postgraduate	5.0	4.0	8.4	15.5
Age[a]				
Under 18	9.0		23.4	19.6
18-24				
25-34	24.0		34.6	36.4
35-44	22.8			
45-54	17.9		38.3	41.3
55-64	14.8			
65+	11.4		3.7	2.8
Occupation[a]				
Professional	14.5	16.0	17.7	24.6
Managerial and sales	15.5	15.5	21.6	27.3
Clerical	21.0	18.5	19.6	20.1
Craftsman	11.5	13.5	4.6	2.1
Operator	14.5	14.5	4.3	4.1
Workman/laborer	10.0	8.5	8.4	7.7
Service	14.0	13.1	14.1	14.8
Income[a]				
Up to $4,999	19.0	16.0	5.0	5.0
$5,000-$9,999	24.0	20.5	16.4	16.0
$10,000-$14,999	22.0	19.5	21.4	20.5
$15,000-$19,999	14.5	15.5	19.4	21.5
$20,000-$24,999	9.0	13.5	13.0	17.0
$25,000-$29,999	11.0	15.0	23.0	20.0
$40,000 and over				
Perceived social class[c]				
Lower		8.0		8.0
Working		44.0		44.1
Middle		43.0		39.6
Upper		2.0		6.3
No such thing		1.0		2.0
No opinion		1.0		

Note: National probability data are reported in this table only when they
were collected at approximately the time of the longitudinal study and only if
question wording was very similar. Because of these requirements, sometimes
no comparable data were found.

Sources: [a]National probability data from General Social Surveys, 1972-
1978: Cumulative Codebook, National Opinion Research Center, University of
Chicago, July 1978.

[b]National probability data source: The General Mills American Family
Report 1974-1975 conducted by Yankelovich, Skelly, and White, Inc. Data
tape was obtained from the Social Science Data Center, The University of
Connecticut, Storrs, Connecticut.

[c]National probability data source: CBS News and New York Times
Polls, April 1978.

TABLE 4.4

Longitudinal Impact of Stagflation on Consumers, 1976 and 1978
(percent)

Stagflation Means	Strongly Agree 1976	Strongly Agree 1978	Agree 1976	Agree 1978	Somewhat Agree 1976	Somewhat Agree 1978	Somewhat Disagree 1976	Somewhat Disagree 1978	Disagree 1976	Disagree 1978	Strongly Disagree 1976	Strongly Disagree 1978	No Answer/Don't Know 1976	No Answer/Don't Know 1978	Total 1976[a]	Total 1978[b]
Prices																
Paying higher prices for products and services	58.7	54.1	31.8	33.2	7.7	9.2	0.5	1.4	0.6	1.4	0.4	0.2	0.3	0.4	100.0	100.0
Prices will be a lot higher in the future	27.7	36.3	40.0	39.7	24.0	17.4	4.3	2.7	2.9	2.8	0.1	0.3	1.0	0.8	100.0	100.0
Products																
There are more low-quality products in the market	27.7	24.5	28.4	28.6	19.4	21.3	10.2	11.7	9.2	8.9	2.4	3.2	2.7	1.8	100.0	100.0
There are more new products in the market	10.0	17.4	33.8	34.1	21.4	18.5	15.1	13.1	11.6	10.9	4.6	2.4	3.5	3.5	100.0	100.0
Product variety is decreasing	6.7	3.8	9.8	12.3	13.6	18.3	21.3	22.7	37.2	32.4	8.8	6.8	2.6	3.7	100.0	100.0
I must buy less of everything	12.6	9.8	22.8	18.5	24.0	25.4	16.7	19.8	18.5	21.1	3.0	3.9	2.3	1.4	100.0	100.0
I must delay purchase of durable goods	16.3	13.5	25.1	24.5	27.0	25.5	10.4	13.7	12.8	18.2	2.4	2.4	6.1	2.3	100.0	100.0
Promotion																
There is more advertising on television	10.0	8.4	28.8	29.2	21.5	24.8	32.8	28.6	2.0	4.5	0.9	1.3	4.0	3.2	100.0	100.0
There are more cents-off coupons in newspapers	17.2	12.6	19.6	22.0	16.4	26.1	40.0	32.5	4.8	3.8	1.2	2.1	0.8	1.0	100.0	100.0
Other																
It's harder to make ends meet	35.1	34.4	35.2	32.1	20.6	20.8	4.1	7.0	1.9	3.5	2.3	0.7	0.8	1.6	100.0	100.0
It's harder to make financial plans	26.3	21.3	35.0	32.4	22.2	23.6	7.1	10.2	5.3	9.4	0.7	1.2	3.3	1.9	100.0	100.0
I must work harder to be able to afford my present way of life	20.0	18.7	25.4	25.1	18.6	22.5	8.9	10.2	13.9	14.2	2.9	2.3	10.2	7.0	100.0	100.0
As a consumer I am more frustrated than I used to be	22.6	15.2	25.5	28.3	27.3	25.8	9.8	12.9	9.7	12.8	2.6	2.0	2.7	3.0	100.0	100.0
As a person I am less happy than I used to be	9.8	6.0	13.6	7.6	18.0	15.1	11.7	17.1	25.5	28.4	10.9	15.4	10.5	10.3	100.0	100.0

[a]N = 969.
[b]N = 916.

Source: Compiled by the author.

and the expectation by over 91 percent of the two samples that prices will be higher in the future, there also came the idea that one must buy less of everything (59.4 percent and 53.7 percent in 1976 and 1978, respectively and even a greater agreement that one must delay the purchase of durable goods (68.4 percent and 63.4 percent in 1976 and 1978, respectively).*

To cope with stagflation, over half of the 1976 and 1978 samples understood that they would have to spend more time shopping and to try to obtain products through wholesale outlets. Similarly, over 50 percent of the 1976 sample and over 60 percent of the 1978 sample perceived an increase in promotional tactics via television and cents-off coupons during stagflation.

Perhaps more important are the findings that as a result of stagflation:

An overwhelming majority of consumers (90.9 percent in 1976 and 87.3 percent in 1978) found it hard to make ends meet or to make financial plans (75.7 percent and 87.3 percent in 1976 and 1978, respectively)

Two-thirds of the 1976 and 1978 samples agreed that they must work harder to be able to afford their present life-style

More than two-thirds of the consumer samples (75.4 percent and 69.3 percent of the 1976 and 1978 samples, respectively) agreed that as consumers they were more frustrated than they used to be

As individuals 41.4 percent of the 1976 sample and 28.7 percent of the 1978 sample reported that they were less happy than they had been before the economic stagflation.

Although the impact of stagflation has been rather drastic, as measured in both 1976 and 1978, differences in scope and depth nevertheless exist. Most notable was the low unemployment rate of the 1978 sample (5.6 percent) relative to the unemployment rate of 1976 (8.0 percent), which understandably resulted in higher mean family income (approximately $16,000 and $19,000 in the 1976 and 1978 samples, respectively). These factors may help to explain other differences between the two samples: a higher percentage reporting no effect of stagflation in 1978 (15.2 percent) relative to 1976

---

*Percentages in this discussion and thereafter, unless otherwise stated, represent the summation of the following response categories: "strongly agree," "agree," and "somewhat agree." Discrepancies in response distribution among these categories in 1976 and 1978 are discussed later in this chapter.

(3.3 percent); and a much smaller percentage reporting a negative impact of stagflation on their personal happiness in 1978 (28.7 percent) relative to 1976 (41.4 percent).

Impact on Consumers

The post-stagflation consumer is clearly a consumer who has changed his or her habits and preferences and has come to judge products and services in a new manner. As can be seen in Table 4.5, over 65 percent of the two samples reported that stagflation had made them change their consumption preferences, and over 75 percent reported that stagflation was responsible for their judging products and services in a new way. Examples of such changes in consumer behavior are shown below (percentages for 1976 and 1978, respectively).

More comparison shopping: 88.9 percent, 85.6 percent
Shopping for "specials" and bargains: 83.9 percent, 81.8 percent
Looking for cheaper products (such as private labels): 60.9 percent, 59.7 percent
Buying more products through wholesale outlets: 56.3 percent, 55.5 percent
Becoming less wasteful: 86.7 percent, 85.0 percent
Spending more time (on the average) shopping: 71.4 percent, 54.3 percent
Repairing durable goods rather than replacing them: 81.0 percent, 76.8 percent
Looking for more durability when shopping for durable goods: 87.0 percent, 87.6 percent
Value fuel economy in cars: 82.3 percent, 81.2 percent.

These changes may be explained by the following inferential process: stagflation expresses itself by higher prices and a higher unemployment rate, which means smaller real or disposable income; to minimize the impact of rising prices on their welfare, consumers take more time shopping, and shop comparatively and seriously; and when they finally decide to purchase a product, they look for more value for their scarce resources. For example, once they decide to buy cars, fuel economy and durability become very important.

In addition to changes in decision making and shopping habits, consumers used two complementary measures to minimize the impact of stagflation on their life-styles: they saved less, and they used more credit. Arguments about financial matters may constitute

TABLE 4.5

Longitudinal Impact of Stagflation, 1976 and 1978
(percent)

Area and Type of Impact	Agree Strongly 1976	1978	Agree 1976	1978	Somewhat Agree 1976	1978	Somewhat Disagree 1976	1978	Disagree 1976	1978	Strongly Disagree 1976	1978	No Answer/ Don't Know 1976	1978	Total 1976[a]	1978[b]
Consumer behavior																
As a consumer I have changed my habits and preferences	12.3	12.0	25.0	25.7	28.6	28.3	12.3	12.4	16.0	16.0	3.9	4.5	2.0	1.1	100.0	
Judge products and services in a new way	16.8	13.1	33.8	38.2	27.2	25.5	7.8	10.0	9.4	8.5	2.1	1.2	2.8	3.5	100.0	100.0
Realize that I can't really improve my economic position	11.8	6.1	12.5	8.1	14.0	12.1	15.3	17.6	26.7	30.8	18.4	22.7	2.1	2.4	100.0	
More of a comparison shopper	32.0	25.5	35.8	39.1	21.1	21.0	3.3	5.2	5.8	6.7	0.7	1.1	1.0	1.4	100.0	100.0
Less wasteful	26.8	19.9	38.7	41.5	21.2	23.6	4.9	6.6	5.3	6.0	1.2	0.8	2.0	1.6	100.0	100.0
Shop for "specials" and bargains	29.7	22.4	28.9	33.9	25.3	25.5	6.4	8.5	6.3	6.5	2.1	1.5	2.2	1.6	100.0	100.0
Budget myself	24.0	18.1	29.8	33.4	25.4	25.4	8.0	8.2	7.9	9.8	2.3	2.4	2.6	2.6	100.0	100.0
Look for cheaper products (such as private labels)	14.5	10.2	21.1	24.4	25.3	25.1	13.2	14.1	17.4	17.0	5.1	6.1	3.3	1.2	100.0	
Buy more products through wholesale outlets (clothes, appliances)	13.1	12.5	23.1	22.3	20.1	20.7	12.3	12.7	19.6	20.5	4.7	5.4	7.2	5.9	100.0	
Repair durable goods rather than replace them	18.6	13.1	36.4	38.2	26.0	25.5	6.5	10.0	7.2	8.5	1.4	1.2	3.8	3.5	100.0	
Look for more durability when shopping for durable goods	28.3	24.7	39.2	43.9	19.5	20.0	3.3	4.3	5.2	4.6	1.3	1.2	3.2	1.3	100.0	
Spend more time (on the average) shopping	13.7	8.1	27.1	23.1	20.6	23.1	9.3	16.0	18.8	21.8	5.4	5.0	5.2	3.0	100.0	100.0
Pay my bills late	17.0	5.3	10.5	8.7	10.7	14.1	12.0	15.4	32.6	33.2	19.4	19.3	7.8	3.5	100.0	100.0
Put off car repairs (among car owners)	9.0	5.0	12.2	10.8	13.3	19.4	10.4	14.4	33.3	35.5	19.8	14.0	2.0	1.6	100.0	
Value fuel economy in cars (among car owners)	24.6	18.3	37.6	39.7	20.1	23.2	5.1	8.2	9.5	7.5	1.9	2.4	1.2	0.7	100.0	

The table below records, for each statement, two response distributions (sample a = 1976, N = 969; sample b = 1978, N = 916) across seven unlabeled response categories plus a total. Percentages are rounded.

Statement	Sample	1	2	3	4	5	6	7	Total
Unemployment									
Become insecure about my job	a	9.5	10.6	15.9	10.9	26.7	10.2	16.1	100.0
	b	6.1	5.9	10.9	12.6	34.2	16.0	14.1	100.0
I get paid what I am worth	a	10.2	19.0	16.1	16.7	17.3	16.7	13.8	100.0
	b	6.3	18.3	16.7	8.6	18.9	17.1	14.1	100.0
Job security more important than money	a	15.4	22.8	27.0	6.9	15.8	8.1	3.9	100.0
	b	7.7	15.8	25.0	5.9	22.8	17.0	5.5	100.0
Political									
Lose faith in the government	a	23.3	16.6	24.3	11.9	15.1	6.1	2.7	100.0
	b	11.3	18.6	23.0	14.6	22.0	8.4	2.1	100.0
By and large, I think politicians are doing a good job of solving our problems	a	3.1	3.2	7.6	22.8	28.4	28.5	6.3	100.0
	b	1.6	4.2	11.0	28.9	29.3	16.9	8.0	100.0
Government is to blame for the way prices keep going up	a	21.7	24.4	27.8	9.7	5.3	2.1	8.4	100.0
	b	10.3	13.1	25.5	17.2	14.7	4.8	14.3	100.0
The government should control prices and profits	a	21.9	18.2	18.3	11.4	12.0	7.9	9.9	100.0
	b	10.1	11.2	14.2	16.6	18.5	18.3	11.2	100.0
Lose faith in the economy	a	23.0	20.0	26.2	12.4	12.8	3.6	1.9	100.0
	b	15.5	19.2	22.1	19.6	16.5	5.6	1.5	100.0
Big companies are to blame for the way prices keep going up	a	21.7	24.4	27.8	9.7	5.3	2.1	8.4	100.0
	b	10.3	13.3	25.5	17.2	14.7	4.8	13.6	100.0
Family									
I weigh purchase decisions with my spouse more than I used to (for married respondents)	a	20.0	29.0	22.4	10.6	12.8	2.8	2.4	100.0
	b	15.0	36.3	18.1	10.7	17.2	2.2	0.5	100.0
More arguments about financial matters	a	8.0	14.0	21.6	13.0	24.6	9.0	9.8	100.0
	b	3.5	13.8	18.5	14.5	32.5	12.9	4.3	100.0
Our family is too heavily in debt today	a	6.1	7.0	12.9	15.4	31.1	21.5	6.1	100.0
	b	3.8	8.5	12.7	18.8	31.3	20.2	4.6	100.0
No matter how fast our income goes up, we never seem to get ahead	a	19.4	17.2	25.2	14.3	13.2	4.9	5.8	100.0
	b	13.3	21.0	22.4	19.0	14.3	5.6	4.4	100.0
Visit family and friends more often	a	8.4	18.4	17.9	16.9	23.9	4.7	9.8	100.0
	b	5.5	14.4	18.9	19.1	27.0	8.0	7.0	100.0
Individuals									
I am less happy than I used to be	a	9.8	13.6	18.0	11.7	25.5	10.9	10.5	100.0
	b	6.0	7.6	15.1	17.1	28.4	15.4	10.3	100.0
My life is anxiety-ridden	a	7.5	9.4	19.3	18.6	26.3	12.8	6.1	100.0
	b	4.7	6.1	16.9	17.1	33.9	17.1	4.3	100.0

Notes: Percentages are rounded.

Unemployment in 1976 was 8 percent (7.7 percent nationally); in 1978, 5.6 percent (6 percent nationally).

aN = 969

bN = 916

Source: Compiled by the author.

an integral part of the post-stagflation life-style of consumers:
43.6 percent and 35.8 percent of consumers in 1976 and 1978, respectively, argued about finances more than they did before stagflation.

If the above explanations are accepted at face value, it is possible to conclude that changes in consumer behavior due to stagflation reaffirm some of the basic assumptions of consumer behavior
theories: that consumers are utilitarian, rational, and consistent.

Impact on Employment

Because of stagflation many consumers became insecure
about their jobs (36.0 percent in 1976 and 22.9 percent in 1978),
and as a result they valued job security more than money (65.2 percent in 1966 and 48.5 percent in 1978). While the gaps between the
two samples relating to job security can be explained by the relatively low unemployment rate in 1978, the two samples were alike
in that less than half of all consumers surveyed felt proud of their
jobs. For the majority, it seems, a job was only an instrument
for gaining monetary resources.

Political Impact

Economic forces often manifest themselves in political attitudes, but are rarely transformed into political actions. It is believed that the present economic stagflation has had such a strong
impact on political attitudes that there is little question about the
conversion of such attitudes into actions. Because of stagflation
and the way it has been handled, more and more people are critical
of the government and business, and are disillusioned with them.
Such people (percentages for 1976 and 1978, respectively):

Lose faith in government: 64.2 percent, 52.9 percent (Ford and
    Carter administrations)
Lose faith in the economy: 69.2 percent, 56.8 percent (Ford and
    Carter administrations)
Think that government is to blame for the way prices keep going up:
    81.5 percent, 62.1 percent (Ford and Carter administrations)
Think that big companies are to blame for the way prices keep go-
    ing up: 73.9 percent, 58.9 percent
Think that politicians are doing a good job of solving problems:
    13.9 percent, 16.8 percent.

Impact on the Family

Stagflation is associated with increasing arguments about finances among family members (43.6 percent in 1976 and 35.8 percent in 1978), feelings of too much debt (26.0 percent and 25.0 percent, respectively), and inability to get ahead economically (61.8 percent and 56.7 percent, respectively). It is also associated with a change in family role structure toward more joint decision making by husband and wife (71.4 percent in 1976 and 69.4 percent in 1978), either because more spouses have joined the labor force or for purposes of reducing risk. In addition, because of stagflation over half the respondents in both 1976 and 1978 reported that they were spending more time at home.

David Caplovitz reported that 14 percent of his sample (N = 1,955) stated that "inflationary pressures had only made their marriage worse. . . . Furthermore, the greater the impact of inflation and recession the more severe the strain on marriage" (1978, p. 220).

Impact on the Individual

Significantly, respondents seemed determined not to let economic matters, however serious, determine their personal well-being. Thus, when it was suggested that because of the "economic crisis" life had become anxiety-ridden or unhappy, the majority in both 1976 and 1978 disagreed. Only 41.4 percent of the 1976, and 28.7 percent of the 1978, survey reported that they were less happy than they used to be because of stagflation. Consistent with these findings, Caplovitz (1979) reported that about 27 percent of his sample's mental health suffered because of stagflation, and that the greater the impact of stagflation, the greater the damage to mental health.

The conclusion from the above is rather clear: stagflation influenced many facets of life drastically and negatively, thus supporting the proposition that it should not be looked upon in economic terms alone. Rather, it is a sociopolitical problem almost as much as it is an economic problem. Possible sociopolitical implications are the following:

A need for political change, if not a new political order, that was fulfilled only to some extent by the Carter administration
A need for economic change, if not for a new economic system, which, to an even lesser extent, was fulfilled by the Carter administration

A change in family role structure toward more joint decision making
by husband and wife, either because more women have joined the
labor force or for purposes of risk reduction

Avoidance of medical/dental services, which can bring about a less
healthy society

A less altruistic society, giving smaller donations and thus representing a return to "social egotism" or the "lifeboat ethic"

Spending more time at home, which may mean a halt to the increased influence of groups other than the family or immediate
friends in shaping one's values and behavior.

The extent to which adjustments to stagflation were made in
1976 and 1978 is strikingly similar: when one combines the "strongly agree," "agree," and "somewhat agree" columns for 1976 and
1978, the results are very alike in most cases. One can explain
such similarity in the drastic adjustment measures as simply being
the longitudinal adjustments to stagflation: a new breed of consumers that has changed its societal outlook, family role structure,
and social altruism.

However, in spite of these similarities, notable longitudinal
differences nevertheless exist. Because of easing inflation and unemployment, consumers in 1978 were less apt to argue about financial matters (43.6 percent of the 1976 sample and 35.8 percent of
the 1978 sample argued), or feel insecure about their jobs (36.0
percent in 1976 and 22.9 percent in 1978). Also, because of the
changes in presidential leadership, the 1978 consumers did not lose
as much faith in the economy and government as did the consumers
of the 1976 survey.

Perhaps a more meaningful but less noticeable longitudinal
difference is the degree of consumer agreement with the statements
in Table 4.5. As can be seen in that table, consumers surveyed in
1976 tended to use the "strongly agree" response category more
often than did consumers surveyed in 1978, and vice versa for the
"agree" column. This longitudinal difference may be explained as
follows: consumers in 1976 were still in a state of shock from the
extreme economic stagflation of 1974 and 1975 (double-digit inflation and up to 9 percent unemployment); consequently, many of the
changes were carried out in an extreme manner; consumers in 1978
were veterans of more than five years of stagflation, and therefore
reacted in a more balanced, selective way. For such consumers
stagflation was no longer a total shock, but a familiar though un-
comfortable way of life.

The same explanations hold true for data presented in Table
4.4, as well as for other tables in this chapter.

DIFFERENTIAL IMPACT OF STAGFLATION

The extreme impact and adjustment measures taken by most respondents in 1976 and 1978 notwithstanding, it is important to analyze how different consumer groups were influenced by stagflation. To do so, this section examines the adjustment measures, life-styles, and socioeconomic status that characterize consumer groups who were positively, negatively, or neutrally affected by stagflation in 1976 and 1978. Cross-tabulation was used to analyze the findings presented in this section.

The results of such analyses are presented in Tables 4.6 and 4.7. In general, consumers who were negatively affected by stagflation (the majority in both 1976 and 1978) tended to adjust, by choice or otherwise, in a much more drastic manner compared with those who were neutrally or positively affected. Similarly, these negatively affected consumers tended to exhibit a life-style different from those who were affected in a neutral or positive mode.*

Differences in Adjustments

As can be seen from Tables 4.6 and 4.7, consumers who were negatively or positively affected in 1976, and consumers who were negatively, neutrally, or positively affected in 1978, differed significantly in their expectations and purchase behavior.

1976

Negatively affected consumers tended to agree significantly more strongly on the following (see Table 4.6 for a complete list of items and significant differences):

It is harder to make ends meet
I am less happy than I used to be
As a consumer I have changed my habits and preferences
As a consumer I am more frustrated than I used to be
There are fewer new products in the market
Product variety is decreasing

---

*The "neutral" point for 1976 (total 3.3 percent of the respondents) was eliminated from the statistical analyses because its inclusion would have resulted in too many empty cells. Analyzed separately, however, these respondents tended to be rather similar to the positively affected group, in that they tended to utilize the "disagree" pole of the scales more often than the other respondents.

TABLE 4.6

Differential Impact of Stagflation on Consumers, 1976 and 1978

Overall Impact of Stagflation by	1976 (X^2 with 2df=)	1978 (X^2 with 4df=)
Prices will be a lot higher in the future[a]	1.1	7.7‡
It is harder to make ends meet	7.4†	15.8*
I am more careful with money	1.4	26.2*
It is harder to make financial plans	2.1	38.1*
I am less happy than I used to be	18.9*	10.2†
I have to work harder to be able to afford my present way of life	5.3‡	14.3*
I must delay purchases of durable goods	0.2	29.6*
I must buy less of everything	1.7	15.9*
There are more low-quality products in the market than there used to be	1.2	8.1‡
As a consumer I have changed my habits and preferences	8.7*	13.4*
As a consumer I am more frustrated than I used to be	8.8*	19.8*
There are fewer new products in the market	18.8*	7.8‡
I do not take chances with new products any more	34.3*	6.1
The variety of products is decreasing	31.0*	6.0
The recent economic crisis has made me		
More of a comparison shopper	0.0	14.9*
Cut down on luxuries	5.8‡	17.8*
Shop for "specials" and bargains	0.4	24.3*
Budget myself	2.5	16.8*
Lose faith in the economy	7.2†	10.0†
Use more credit	5.7†	6.2
Save less	1.9	18.3*
Drive less	7.9*	4.0
Spend more time at home	10.4*	5.8
Become insecure about my job	5.2‡	9.4†
Argue about financial matters	1.1	10.3†
Look for cheaper products	3.9	21.7*
Dine out less	2.5	21.7*
Visit my family and friends more often	5.8†	2.2
Buy more products through wholesale outlets	2.4	15.9*
Stop giving donations or give smaller ones	20.6*	18.0*
Energy conscious	2.4	11.5†
Repair durable goods rather than replace them	3.8	9.2†

	1976 (X^2 with 2df=)	1978 (X^2 with 4df=)
Spend less on hobbies	11.4*	13.9*
Judge products and services in a new way	4.0	11.6†
Look for more durability in durables	0.0	5.1
Weigh purchase decisions with spouse more than before	10.6*	8.1‡
Spend more time shopping	9.6*	6.8
Pay my bills late	4.0	12.4*
Put off car repairs	8.6*	5.9
Put off medical/dental checkups or treatments	0.3	7.9‡
Become a do-it-yourself person	0.3	14.4*
Spend more time watching TV	20.5*	9.4†
Realize that I can't improve my economic position	21.1*	9.9†
Lose faith in government	1.5	14.0*
Employment[b]	22.0 (4df)*	19.0 (8df)*
Occupation[c]	36.0 (8df)*	19.8 (10df)†
Income[d]	27.8 (7df)*	25.1 (14df)*
Marital status[e]	38.5 (4df)*	5.8 (8df)
Age[f]	32.0 (4df)*	4.6 (8df)
Education[g]	27.1 (3df)*	4.3 (6df)
Race[h]	18.2 (4df)†	21.0 (8df)*
Spouse working (yes, no)	5.1 (1df)*	0.0 (2df)

Note: 1976 impacts are positive or negative; 1978 impacts are positive, negative, or neutral.

*Significant at $P \leq .001$.

†Significant at $P \leq .05$.

‡Significant at $P \leq .10$. That is, there is a confidence level of 99 percent, 95 percent, and 90 percent, respectively, that the groups impacted are truly different in their responses to the above statements.

[a]Scale points (after collapsing): 1. strongly agree, agree, somewhat agree; 2. don't know; 3. somewhat disagree, disagree, strongly disagree.

[b]Employed, unemployed, homemaker, retired, student.

[c]Workman/laborer, operator, craftsman, service, clerical, sales, professional, managerial, other.

[d]$4,999 or less, $5,000-9,000, $10,000-14,999, $15,000-19,999, $20,000-24,999, $25,000-29,999, $30,000-39,999, $40,000 or over.

[e]Single, married, divorced, widowed, separated.

[f]18-24, 25-34, 35-49, 50-64, 65 or over.

[g]Some high school or less, high school, some college, college graduate and beyond.

[h]Black, Caucasian, Oriental, Hispanic, other.

Source: Compiled by the author.

TABLE 4.7

Differential Impact of Stagflation on Consumer Life-Style, 1976 and 1978

Overall Impact of Stagflation, by	1976 (X^2 with 2df=)	1978 (X^2 with 4df=)
Shopping and finances		
Shopping is great fun[a]	6.3[+]	4.3
The worst part of shopping is the high prices	3.9	13.1*
Shopping is a serious business for me	5.9[+]	5.8
A store's own brand is usually just as good as a nationally advertised brand	6.5[+]	10.8[+]
If I had more money, I would spend more on food	13.1*	2.5
Our family is too heavily in debt today	18.0*	9.3[+]
No matter how fast our income goes up, we never seem to get ahead	12.8*	22.0*
Personal and job-related		
My life is anxiety ridden	25.7*	8.3[‡]
Sometimes I feel that we are living on the edge of disaster	5.6[‡]	6.6
I get paid what I am worth	9.1*	12.2*
It is hard to get a good job these days	3.1	8.8[+]
In a job, security is more important than money	14.4*	3.9
I take pride in my job	6.4[+]	3.0
Attitude toward business		
What America needs is more individual initiative	4.6[‡]	3.9
Most big companies are just out for themselves	1.7	9.1[+]
Big companies are to blame for the way prices are going up	3.5	8.9[‡]
Business spends too much lobbying and not enough improving consumer products	0.9	10.4[+]
It makes me mad when I think about how much money people make on second-rate products	6.7[+]	14.1*
Success in business is largely a matter of luck	13.1*	2.3
TV commercials really make sense	22.2*	5.1
Advertising sells a product, often without telling the truth about it	8.5*	11.3[+]
Political attitudes		
I consider myself a member of the silent majority	9.4*	2.5
By and large, I think politicians are doing a good job	12.8*	22.8*
Government is to blame for the way prices keep going up	4.7[‡]	7.6[‡]
The government should control prices and profits	7.8*	4.9

Note: 1976 impacts are positive or negative; 1978 impacts are positive, negative, or neutral.

*Significant at $P \leq .001$.

[+]Significant at $P \leq .05$.

[‡]Significant at $P \leq .10$. That is, there is a confidence level of 99 percent, 95 percent, and 90 percent respectively that the groups impacted are truly different in their responses to the above statements.

[a]Scale points (after collapsing): 1. strongly agree, agree, somewhat agree; 2. don't know; 3. somewhat disagree, disagree, strongly disagree.

Source: Compiled by the author.

Such consumers also agreed more strongly that because of stagflation they did the following:

Cut down on luxuries
Lost faith in the economy
Used more credit
Drove less
Spent more time at home
Became insecure about their jobs
Visited family and friends more often
Spent less on hobbies
Weighed purchase decisions with spouse more than before
Spent more time shopping
Gave smaller donations

1978

Negatively affected consumers tended to agree significantly more strongly than positively or neutrally affected consumers on the following points (see Table 4.6):

Prices will be a lot higher in the future
It is harder to make ends meet
I am more careful with money
It is harder to make financial plans
I am less happy than I used to be
I must buy less of everything
I must delay purchases of durable goods
As a consumer I have changed my habits and preferences
As a consumer I am more frustrated than I used to be

Such consumers also agreed more strongly that due to stagflation, they did the following:

Became more comparative shoppers
Cut down on luxuries
Budgeted themselves
Saved less
Argued about financial matters
Became insecure about their jobs
Looked for cheaper products
Spent less on hobbies
Put off medical or dental checkups or treatments
Lost faith in government

Differences in Life-Styles

Negatively affected consumers in both 1976 and 1978 tended to
agree significantly more strongly about the following psychographic
items concerning shopping, employment, politics, and business (see
Table 4.7).

Our family is too heavily in debt today
No matter how fast our income goes up, we never seem to get ahead
My life is anxiety-ridden
I get paid what I am worth (reverse)
It makes me mad when I think about how much money people make
    on second-rate products
Advertising sells a product, often without telling the truth about it
By and large, politicians are doing a good job (reverse)
Government is to blame for the way prices are going up*

While many of the differences presented in Tables 4.6 and 4.7
and outlined in this section may not be surprising, checking the
socioeconomic status of negatively affected consumers revealed unexpected results. Compared with consumers who were otherwise
affected, negatively affected consumers in both 1976 and 1978 tended
to be mostly middle-class: professionals and managers, middle-
income individuals, and college graduates. Explanations of such
puzzling results seem to be mainly sociopolitical. (Such explanations and their implications for marketing management were discussed in Chapter 3.)

THE LONGITUDINAL IMPACT SIMPLIFIED

In the previous section the impact of stagflation on society,
including variables that might account for the differential impact,
was established. The discussion centered on facets of life that
logically seem different: consumption, employment, family life,
and voter and individual attitudes. As a result the presentation included detailed accounts of many variables relating to the life facet
in question. Although such an approach is fairly conclusive, it can
also be very confusing because the variables are numerous and
often repetitive.

---

*Additional aspects of what accounts for the differences in the
impact of stagflation are discussed in Appendix A.

To simplify the situation and achieve parsimony, the variables relating to the impact of stagflation (altogether more than 50) were reduced in number by using factor analysis. Factor analysis is a statistical technique which is designed to reduce data based on similarities and differences among responses. A factor usually includes several related variables which are said to "load" on that factor. Tables 4.8 and 4.9 include the variables and factor loadings for the 1976 and 1978 samples, respectively. Variables were considered to belong to a factor only if their factor loading was 0.5 or higher, and in almost all cases variables loaded that high on one factor only, that is, belonged clearly to one factor.

As can be seen from Tables 4.8 and 4.9, factor analysis makes it possible to discuss the impact of stagflation in terms of seven factors instead of numerous variables. Factors relating to the impact of stagflation in 1976 are shown below in rank order.

1. Shopping and budgeting, which is concerned with comparison shopping, bargain hunting, and managing money more carefully
2. Car and car repair, which includes three highly related variables: driving less, putting off car repairs, and attaching high value to fuel economy in cars
3. Economic and political attitudes, relating to loss of faith in the economy and government
4. Purchasing and spending, which is concerned with having to buy less of everything, and at the same time to save less
5. Product variety, which includes consumer perception of product variety, and reluctance to take chances with new products
6. Bills and checkups, relating to paying bills late and putting off medical and dental checkups
7. Leisure time, which centers on the impact of stagflation on leisure-time allocation: spending time at home, visiting family and friends, watching television or reading, and spending time on do-it-yourself projects.

Factors emerging from the 1978 data were surprisingly similar to those that emerged from the 1976 data (see Table 4.9). These factors, in rank order, relate to the following:

1. Price and price expectations, and their implications (a new factor; some of its items are included in factor no. 4 of the 1976 data)
2. Economic and political attitudes (factor no. 3 in 1976)
3. Bills and checkups (factor no. 6 in 1976)
4. Purchasing and spending (factor no. 4 in 1976)
5. Product variety (factor no. 5 in 1976)

TABLE 4.8

Factor Analysis of the Impact of Stagflation, 1976

Factor Name and Rank	Variable (Because of Stagflation)	Factor and Factor Loading						
		1	2	3	4	5	6	7
1. Shopping and budgeting	I am more careful with money	.54						
	I am a more comparative shopper	.74						
	I am less wasteful	.66						
	I shop for "specials" and bargains more than before	.64						
	I budget myself	.57						
2. Car and car repair	I value fuel economy in cars		.60					
	I put off car repairs		.62					
	I drive less		.77					
3. Economic and political	I have lost faith in the economy			.68				
	I have lost faith in the government			.67				
4. Purchasing and spending	I must buy less of everything				.62			
	It is harder to make financial plans				.58			
	I must delay purchase of durable goods				.57			
	It is harder to make ends meet				.52			
	I save less				.50			
5. Product variety	There are fewer new products in the market					.71		
	Product variety is decreasing					.70		
	I do not take chances with new products any more					.51		
6. Bills and checkups	I put off medical and dental checkups and treatments						.55	
	I pay my bills late						.50	
7. Leisure time	I spend more time at home							.55
	I visit family and friends more often than I used to							.53
	I spend more time watching television							.52
	I spend more time reading							.50
	I have become a do-it-yourself person							.50

Source: Compiled by the author.

TABLE 4.9

Factor Analysis of the Impact of Stagflation, 1978

Factor Name and Rank	Variable (Because of Stagflation)	Factor and Factor Loading						
		1	2	3	4	5	6	7
1. Price and price expectations	I pay higher prices for products and services	.64						
	It is harder to make ends meet	.63						
	Prices will be a lot higher in the future	.54						
	It is harder to make financial plans	.52						
2. Economic and political	I have lost faith in the government		.72					
	I have lost faith in the economy		.69					
3. Bills and checkups	I put off car repairs			.60				
	I put off medical and dental checkups and treatments			.58				
	I pay my bills late			.55				
4. Purchasing and spending	I must delay purchase of durable goods				.58			
	I dine out less				.58			
	I must buy less of everything				.56			
	I spend less on hobbies				.53			
5. Product variety	There are fewer new products in the market					.77		
	The variety of products is decreasing					.70		
6. Leisure time	I spend more time reading						.60	
	I spend more time at home						.56	
	I spend more time watching television						.51	
7. Shopping and budgeting	I do more comparison shopping							.71
	I shop for "specials" and bargains more than before							.67
	I am less wasteful							.66
	I budget myself							.57
	I cut down on luxuries							.50

Source: Compiled by the author.

6. Leisure time (factor no. 7 in 1976)
7. Shopping and budgeting (factor no. 1 in 1976)

Compressing the impact of stagflation into a smaller number of factors, as was done above, not only enables the reader to understand the results more easily, but also makes it possible to compare the results and to discern trends. Thus, although similar factors emerged in both 1976 and 1978, it is worthwhile to point out two important differences or trends. The first centers on the growing importance that consumers attached to prices, expectation about future prices, and the resulting perceptions about financial plans and the ability to make ends meet. An indication of this growing importance lies in the fact that it appeared as the first factor in the 1978 data— that is, the factor that, relative to each of the others, explained the greatest amount of variance among respondents. After the high rates of inflation, it is understandable (and quite rational on the part of the consumer) that prices headed the factor list.

Another trend is indicated in the ranking of the "economic and political attitudes" factor. Having placed third in 1976 and second in 1978, it shows the growing frustration with the economy and the government, and possibly implies readiness of consumers to take the economic initiative back from the government.

THE DIFFERENTIAL IMPACT SIMPLIFIED

To show differences among those who in general were positively, neutrally, and negatively influenced by stagflation, it is possible to examine such differences among the factors that emerged from the factor analysis (see Tables 4.8 and 4.9). To do so, the seven factors conceived as new variables are cross-tabulated by the overall impact of stagflation and by socioeconomic variables.

The results of such analysis are almost identical to those appearing in Tables 4.6 and 4.7, and therefore are not repeated.

CONCLUSIONS

The extreme impact on most consumers notwithstanding, the findings thus far in this chapter indicate the growing importance of consumer psychology variables relative to such traditionally important socioeconomic variables as occupation, age, and race in explaining the variance among differently affected consumers. This seems to lend support to George Katona's classic report that consumers' attitudes and expectations are often more important than

disposable income in explaining consumer spending (Katona 1960,
1964; Katona, Strumpel, and Zahn 1971).

Reaching far beyond the basic behavioral economic thesis,
however, is the fact that stagflation seems to affect most aspects
of human behavior, including personal happiness, life-style, and
societal and political roles. Thus, one can outline the following
implications and research areas concerning consumer behavior during periods of stagflation:

1. Behavioral economics becomes of utmost importance when economics is more salient in consumer well-being—that is, during
   periods of stagflation. In fact, as consumer behavior in the
   1970s defied many of the prescriptions of traditional economic
   theory, there emerged a growing trend to modify such theory by
   introducing psychological or behavioral variables. Consistent
   with this, the emerging "rational expectations" school of thought
   argues that consumer behavior is largely determined by expectations concerning the economy and economic policy, and not
   necessarily by present income (Gruzzardi 1978).
2. Consequently, integrating economic dimensions and their psychological manifestations into the conceptualizations of consumer
   behavior increases the degree of verisimilitude of such conceptualizations. It is meaningful to note here that in the past, general theories of consumer behavior have given only cursory
   treatment to consumer economics (see, for example, Engel,
   Kollat, and Blackwell 1968; Howard and Sheth 1969; Nicosia 1966).
   It is logical to assume that integrating salient economic variables,
   such as various aspects of stagflation, would improve future at-
   tempts to construct consumer behavior theories that are not only
   descriptive and explanatory, but also predictive.
3. Consistent with (2), researching consumer behavior during stagflation contributes to the knowledge of consumer behavior in important situations rarely experienced before in such degree or
   scope. Examples of such research avenues are the following:
   Exactly what constitutes value to the consumer and what determines which type of consumers enters or leaves the various
   parts of the demand curve? What strategies are available to
   consumers that can help them minimize the impact of stagflation
   (such as increasing family participation in the work force and
   changing decisions about product mix, shopping tactics, recep-
   tiveness to promotion and coupons, and price bargaining)? This
   last point heightens the importance of researching consumer-
   business dynamics during stagflation.
4. As suggested in Chapter 1, the "stagnation thesis" holds that
   stagflation is a phenomenon encompassing most facets of life.

Consequently, researching how consumers behave during stagflation contributes to disciplines such as economics, social psychology, and political economy, from which consumer behavior theories have borrowed extensively.

MARKETING IMPLICATIONS

Although it is generally correct to argue that post-stagflation consumers constitute a new breed of consumers whose reactions to the marketing mix may be utterly different from those of pre-stagflation consumers, such a description is much more fitting for those affected by stagflation in an extreme manner.* Such consumers try very hard to cut costs and maintain value through comparison shopping, bargain hunting, buying through wholesale outlets, dining out less, and spending less on health care, yet they may find that ends do not meet. These consumers represent rather large segments with profitable marketing potential and opportunities. Examples of such marketing opportunities are shown below:

1. In general, because of the drastically negative impact of stagflation, consumers become highly value-minded, and therefore may be attracted by products that are so promoted.
2. Consistent with the above, products may be downgraded or cheaper products that still represent good value to consumers may be produced. This does not mean that all inexpensive products will do well; only products for which a potentially strong demand does not materialize because of high prices will do so. In such a stagflation environment, incidentally, five-and-dime stores may have growth problems because to many consumers they are associated with inexpensive products lacking in value.
3. New financial services or management may be profitably offered to consumers to help them make ends meet. This proposition is supported by high profit rates of the banking industry in the United States as well as in other countries experiencing high degrees of stagflation.

---

*Since most consumers were negatively influenced by stagflation, the rest of the discussion focuses on them. Appendix A examines statistical models that may describe the overall impact of stagflation and consumer adjustments parsimoniously. Marketing opportunities discussed below are based in part on findings reported in Appendix A.

4. Channel outlets may be adjusted to consumers looking for retail value at wholesale prices. The proliferation of cut-rate stores, the developing limited-assortment stores, and the growing number of independent street vendors are but a few examples.
5. The marketing mix in the health care industry may be modified to control costs; otherwise demand for nonemergency medical treatment may decrease. Permitting doctors to advertise may control such cost by increasing competition.
6. The marketing mix in the restaurant business may be modified to appeal to the small-budget consumer. For example, introducing "fast-food" merchandising techniques and "specials" may attract more customers, and thus increase profit by increasing volume.
7. Consumers positively affected by stagflation may constitute a distinct market segment representing additional marketing opportunities.

Except for the last point, the target group(s) for the above marketing opportunities are those negatively affected by stagflation. As stated before, such consumers tend to be middle-class people or affluent consumers—the target group of many products and services. Although this last statement may contradict some myths and stereotypes, it is based on extensive research findings (see Chapter 3).

CONSUMER AND MARKETING MANAGEMENT
DURING STAGFLATION

The impact of stagflation on marketing-mix decisions, and the resulting adjustments by marketing management, were discussed at great length and backed by survey data in Chapter 2. In the discussion of how stagflation influences marketing management decisions concerning target consumers, product, price, promotion, and place, it was shown that all of these decision areas were drastically affected, though not equally so. As can be seen in Table 2.2, taking the "very much" or "much" (impact) columns to indicate drastic effects, the rank order was price (highest), product, promotion, and place (lowest). (See "The Effects of Stagflation" in Chapter 2.)

The effects of stagflation on consumers were drastic, too. As shown in Table 4.4, most consumers were negatively affected by the marketing mix during stagflation. In both 1976 and 1978 they experienced high prices and expected more of the same in the future; they also realized that they must curb consumption, and in order to make ends meet they redeemed cents-off coupons in growing numbers and looked for wholesale outlets.

A comparison of Tables 2.2 and 4.4 shows a very interesting parallel: that stagflation has influenced both marketing management and consumers along similarly ranked economic factors: price, product, promotion, and place. Both marketing management and the consumers have been most affected by price variables, and least affected by place variables. This lends support to a suggestion made in Chapter 2 that economically the nature of stagflation influences price more than it influences other components of the marketing mix. It can also be argued that as a result of the impact on prices, product offerings are the next to change, followed by promotion and place decisions.

Comparatively, how did marketing management and the consumers adjust to stagflation? A comparison of Tables 2.3 and 4.5 offers some insights. Table 2.3 shows that most drastic marketing-mix adjustments were made in the area of pricing and fewest in the areas of promotion and place. This is in line with the perceived impact of stagflation on the marketing mix (see Table 2.2).

Adjustments made by consumers to changes in the marketing mix are reported in the "Consumer Behavior" section of Table 4.5. That table reveals that in both 1976 and 1978 most adjustments by consumers were made in the area of price, and fewest in the areas of place and promotion.

A comparison between Tables 2.3 and 4.3 shows that marketing management and consumers adjusted themselves along similarly ranked factors, placing price and product ahead of promotion and place.

A schematic summary of the impact of, and of adjustments to, stagflation by marketing management and consumers along price, product, promotion, and place as discussed above appears in Table 4.10. It assigns "4" to the most important group of variables, "3" to the next most important group of variables, and so forth; "1" is assigned to the least important group of variables. As can be seen, the impact on marketing management and consumers, and the resulting adjustments, are almost identical. Except for the fact that compared with marketing management, consumers adjusted more often by changing outlets in which they purchased than by taking advantage of sales promotion, and other factors, there is little discernible difference between the rank orderings summarized in Table 4.10.

SUMMARY AND CONCLUSIONS

In this chapter the longitudinal impact of stagflation on consumers, and consumers' resulting coping strategies, were discussed.

TABLE 4.10

Impact of and Adjustments to Stagflation

	Price Variables	Product Variables	Promotion Variables	Place Variables
Impact on[a]				
Marketing management	4[b]	3	2	1
Consumers	4	3	2	1
Adjustments by[c]				
Marketing management	4	3	2	1
Consumers	4	3	2	1

[a]Based on rank ordering of the summations of columns 1 and 2 in Tables 2.2 and 4.4.

[b]A score of 4 represents the highest score, and indicates that the impact (or the adjustments) was (were) highest. A score of 1 represents the least impact and fewest adjustments.

[c]Based on rank ordering of the summations of columns 1 and 2 in Tables 2.3 and 4.5.

Source: Compiled by the author.

The discussion clearly suggests that stagflation has brought about a new breed of consumers whose decision-making process and preferences have changed drastically. Consistent with this, Avichai Shuv-Ami (1979) suggests that because of stagflation, the structure of the consumer attitude has changed. Therefore, profitable opportunities for marketing management may result from better understanding of the post-stagflation consumer and his or her modified attitude structure.

Furthermore, it has been suggested in this chapter that stagflation has affected life-styles as well as political attitudes and social relations. In this respect stagflation may be a societal rather than only an economic phenomenon. Consequently, marketing managers should study not only the business aspects of stagflation, but also its social impact and ramifications.

Finally, in comparing those negatively and positively affected by stagflation, it was found that middle-class consumers report more negative impact than do other classes. (This finding was tested and analyzed more carefully in Chapter 3.)

REFERENCES

Bureau of Economics and Statistics. 1979. Handbook of Basic Economic Statistics. Washington, D.C.: U.S. Government Printing Office.

CBS/New York Times Polls. 1978. New York: CBS. April.

Caplovitz, D. 1979. Making Ends Meet: How Families Cope with Inflation and Recession. Beverly Hills, Calif.: Sage.

Data Resources, Inc. 1978. Consumer Business Review. Boston, Mass.

Davis, J. A., T. W. Smith, and E. B. Stephenson. 1978. General Social Surveys, 1972-1978: Cumulative Codebook. Chicago: National Research Center, University of Chicago.

Dullea, G. 1978. "Those Upwardly Mobile Street Peddlers." New York Times, December 11, p. D13.

Engel, J., D. R. Kollat, and R. D. Blackwell. 1968. Consumer Behavior. New York: Holt, Rinehart and Winston.

Gruzzardi, W., Jr. 1978. "The New Down-to-Earth Economics." Fortune, December 31, pp. 72-79.

Gurin, G., and P. Gurin. 1976. "Personal Efficacy and the Ideology of Individual Responsibility." In Economic Means for Human Needs: Social Indicators of Well-Being and Discontent, edited by B. Strumpel, pp. 131-58. Ann Arbor, Mich.: Survey Research Center.

Hirsch, F. 1978. Social Limits to Growth. Cambridge, Mass.: Harvard University Press.

Howard, J. A., and J. N. Sheth. 1969. The Theory of Buyer Behavior. New York: Wiley.

Katona, G. 1960. The Powerful Consumer. New York: McGraw-Hill.

_____. 1964. The Mass Consumption Society. New York: McGraw-Hill.

_____. 1974. "Psychology and Consumer Economics." Journal of Consumer Research 1, no. 1 (June): 1-2.

_____. 1975. Psychological Economics. Amsterdam.

Katona, G., B. Strumpel, and E. Zahn. 1971. Aspirations and Affluence. New York: McGraw-Hill.

Kelley, E. J., and L. R. Scheewe. 1975. "Buyer Behavior in a Stagflation/Shortages Economy." Journal of Marketing 39 (April): 44-50.

Kunreuther, H., and P. Slovic. 1978. "Economics, Psychology, and Protective Behavior." Proceedings of the American Economic Association 69: 64-69.

Li, J. 1964. Statistical Inference. Vol. 2. Ann Arbor, Mich.: Edwards Bros.

Morgan, J. N. 1978. "Multiple Motives, Group Decisions, Uncertainty, Ignorance, and Confusion: A Realistic Economics of the Consumer Requires Some Psychology." American Economic Review Proceedings 68, no. 2 (May): 58-62.

National Conference Board. 1978. "Consumer Attitudes and Buying Plans." A Monthly Report, November.

Nation's Business. 1975. "Why Consumer Attitudes Matter More Than Economics." Nation's Business 30, no. 9 (September): 34-38.

Newsweek. 1978. "The Inflation Surge: Special Report." May 29, pp. 68-82.

Nicosia, F. M. 1966. Consumer Decision Processes: Marketing and Advertising Implications. Englewood Cliffs, N.J.: Prentice-Hall.

Pfaff, A. B. 1976. "The Quality of Consumption." In Economic Means for Human Needs: Social Indicators of Well-Being and Discontent, edited by B. Strumpel, pp. 187-218. Ann Arbor, Mich.: Survey Research Center.

Poser, G., and Z. E. Shipchandler. 1977. "Impact of Inflation on Consumer Life Style." Paper presented at the 13th CIRET Conference, Munich.

Robock, S. H. 1972. "We Can Live with Inflation." Harvard Business Review 50, no. 6: 20-44.

Shuv-Ami, A. 1979. "Buyers of No-Name Grocery Products in a Period of Stagflation." Working paper, Graduate School of Business, Baruch College.

Strumpel, B. 1973. "Economic Life-Styles, Values and Subjective Welfare—An Empirical Approach." In Family Economic Behavior, edited by E. B. Lippincott, pp. 69-125. Philadelphia: J. P. Lippincott.

_____. 1974. "Economic Well Being as an Object of Social Well Being." In The Selective Elements of Well Being, edited by B. Strumpel. Paris: OECD.

_____, ed. 1976a. Economic Means for Human Needs: Social Indicators of Well-Being and Discontent. Ann Arbor, Mich.: Survey Research Center.

_____. 1976b. "Introduction and Model." In Economic Means for Human Needs: Social Indicators of Well-Being and Discontent, pp. 1-12.

_____. 1976c. "Economic Deprivation and Societal Discontent." In Economic Means for Human Needs: Social Indicators of Well-Being and Discontent, pp. 219-48.

U.S. Department of Health, Education and Welfare, Social Security
    Administration. 1976. Social Security Bulletin. April.

U.S. Department of Labor, Bureau of Labor Statistics. 1975.
    Handbook of Labor Statistics. Ref. ed. Washington, D.C.:
    U.S. Government Printing Office.

_____. 1979. News. Washington, D.C.: U.S. Government Print-
    ing Office. January 17, 1979.

Wachtel, W. H., and P. Adelshein. 1977. "How Recession Feeds
    Inflation: Price Markups in Concentrated Economy." Challenge
    20 (September-October): 6-13.

Yankelovich, Skelly, and White, Inc. 1975. The General Mills
    American Family Report. Minneapolis: General Mills, Inc.

5
MARKETING MANAGEMENT:
ADAPTING TO CONSUMER BEHAVIOR
AND GOVERNMENT REGULATIONS

As has been shown in Chapters 2-4, stagflation represents drastic changes in the economic environment that affect marketing management, the consumer, and economic policy. Stagnant growth and high rates of unemployment have been affecting marketers, consumers, and policy makers since 1973, and their responses have, of course, affected the economic environment. These inter-dependencies are depicted in Figure 5.1. Stagflation influences policy makers, consumers, and marketing management, and is in turn influenced by them. Also actions taken by each of those three groups affect and are affected by actions of the other two groups. Furthermore, while the economic environment in Figure 5.1 is viewed as the independent variable originating the impact, it is conceptually just as valid to conceive each of the three groups as the independent variable affecting the other two groups and the economic environment.

Since the present work focuses to a large degree on marketing management, the view taken in this chapter is concerned with the methods that marketing management can use to control the impact of stagflation. However, this is a particularly difficult task because such control would require marketing management to have meaningful control over consumer decisions and economic policies. That, of course, is not the case. Both consumer decisions and economic policies are noncontrollable variables from marketing management's point of view. Consequently, all that marketing management can do in such a situation is adapt to the changing consumer and economic policies, and take advantage of new opportunities created by them.

In the rest of this chapter, changes in consumer behavior and economic policy making that result from stagflation will be summarized, and marketing management adaptation strategies to such changes will be discussed. However, unlike Chapter 2, where the focus is on the short run, long-run strategic adjustments are the main focus of the present chapter.

FIGURE 5.1

The Relationships among Stagflation, Economic Policy,
Consumers, and Marketing Management

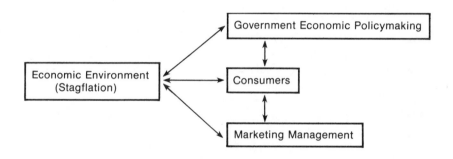

Source: Constructed by the author.

THE POST-STAGFLATION ERA

Stagflation was probably the single most important economic factor in the 1970s. It affected most people negatively, both economically and psychologically. Economically, real income was stagnant or declined while real prices of such necessities as food, transportation, and medical care rose faster than the other, presumably "luxury," components of the Consumer Price Index. As a result, more and more middle-class people were forced to spend a greater share of their income on necessities, and thus to join the ranks of the poor, who traditionally spend the bulk of their income on necessities. The net result was a new class—"the middle-class poor"—which social scientists will study for years to come.

Psychologically, stagflation made the public more erratic, so that small changes in the perceived degree of stagflation triggered increasingly drastic adjustment measures (see Appendix A). Furthermore, stagflation seemed to sharpen social and political conflicts.

All these factors have reshaped people in their roles as consumers, employees, family members, voters, and individuals. Consequently the emerging post-stagflation society is quite different from the pre-stagflation society, and as such will require many marketing-management adjustments.

Although stagflation is not over yet, it is nevertheless possible to point out some important characteristics of the emerging post-stagflation society. This is because of what has been learned from experience with stagflation and because of the author's longitudinal research, started in 1975.

Probably the most important change characterizing the post-stagflation consumer is a new set of values and attitudes guiding his or her behavior not only as a consumer, but also as an individual, voter, employee, and family member. What seems to emerge is a new social order that includes—by definition—changes in consumer behavior, political behavior, and various aspects of social behavior, such as family role structure. Such changes, in turn, have important implications for marketing-management strategies. Table 5.1 presents the characteristics of people in the post-stagflation era and their resulting implications for marketing strategies. These changes and implications are discussed in more detail below.

The Post-Stagflation Consumer

Indications are very strong that the emerging consumer is one whose motives, values, attitudes, and expectations have changed drastically. Such changes, of course, require many changes by marketing management, if profit making through consumer satisfaction is desirable. More specifically, consumer motives in most cases have become more rational. As real disposable income has become stagnant or declined, consumers have become much more careful about spending their limited resources. They examine their product needs carefully and make decisions based on rational, "quantifiable" motives. Consequently, the psychological or emotional connotations of many products have become less important to many consumers.

Although this does not mean that emotional motives are less important than rational motives across all product categories, it does mean that the reason for purchasing many products has become less emotional and more rational. Durable products, furniture, and other home furnishings seem to have experienced such a change, necessitating corresponding changes in product design and concept, and price, promotion, and distribution strategies. As the rational

TABLE 5.1

Characteristics of the Emerging Post-Stagflation Consumer

Level	Area of Change	Nature of Change	Marketing Implications
Consumer	values attitudes motives expectations	functionalism, simplicity structural changes more rational more stagflation, inflation psychology buy now credit real estate	more rational appeals capitalize on changes product simplification more functionalism take advantage of inflation psychology
	marketing mix price	became most important; impact on: shopping behavior use of credit financial management	price carefully and strategically adjust channels make credit more available and adjust its terms take advantage of needs for financial management
	product	functional attributes more important	readjust products to consumer needs
	promotion	more attention to price functional attributes durability	readjust promotion mix, appeal, schedule, and media

	place	receptivity to modified distribution channels	examine value of channel modification capitalize on receptivity to new channels
Employment	attitudes	less security	examine employees' attitudes
	behavior	more dislike of the job more moonlighting more women working	respond to employees' needs capitalize on the increasing number of women in the labor force take advantage of part-time workers
Family membership	role structure	more joint decision making frequent job changing	reposition the product vis-a-vis the new family role structure
Voter	attitudes	more negative	
	behavior	more negative	
Individual	attitude toward economy	more pessimistic	monitor carefully (changes here normally trigger changes in consumption role)

Source: Compiled by the author.

motives in making decisions concerning most products have increased, so have the emotional motives for buying some products.
Good examples are perfume and other products focusing on "me."
This may have been caused by the increasing pressures to make
decisions rationally and carefully.

Changes in consumer motives result, of course, from a much
more basic change: a change in the consumer's value system.
Stagnant growth not only makes it harder for consumers to achieve
material growth; it also makes them feel high levels of anxiety in
the process of achieving such growth. The result is that a growing
number of consumers question the worth of material growth, and
resort to material simplicity. Related to this are the growing
concern for ecological issues, the desire to return to basics, and
the desire to have a simpler, more humanly scaled life-style.

These new values have produced many attitudinal changes in
consumers, including alterations in their attitude structure. As
was shown in Chapter 4, consumers have changed their attitudes
toward many products and services (see Tables 4.4 and 4.5), as
well as the importance they attach to various product attributes.
For example, economy, functionalism, and durability of durable
goods have become more important as a result of stagflation.

Although such value and attitude changes are not necessarily
shown by all consumers, they nevertheless characterize a growing
number of them. In fact, the rate at which the latter group has
been growing has made some researchers discuss it as a social
movement for "voluntary simplicity."

The stagflation-triggered voluntary simplicity movement is
characterized by five core values.*

1. Material simplicity—that is, simplifying or uncluttering one's
   life as an individual and as a consumer
2. Human scale—that is, scaling down or humanizing one's living
   and working environment. This includes not only the value
   "small is beautiful" (Schumacher 1974), but also a changed attitude toward work life, which thus far has attributed much importance to the production process and little to the human

---

*The voluntary simplicity movement was given that name and
outlined by Richard Gregg as early as 1936 (Elgin and Mitchell
1977a). It was quickly forgotten when World War II broke out, and
reappeared in the 1970s. This appearance-reappearance cycle also
characterizes A. H. Hensen's "stagnant" thesis, which was discussed in Chapter 1.

interaction. Related to this is a change of attitude among many employees and their families toward job transfers

3. Self-determination—that is, the need to have more control over one's life and less dependency on organizations, including business
4. Ecological awareness, resulting in the realization that resources are limited, conservation is needed, and pollution reduction is imperative
5. Personal growth—that is, the desire to free oneself from external clutter and develop one's inner life, both psychologically and spiritually (Elgin and Mitchell 1977a).

In characterizing the voluntary simplifiers, Duane Elgin and Arnold Mitchell (1977a; 1977b) claim that there are different degrees of voluntary simplification, depending on the degree of adoption of life-styles described by voluntary simplicity. Thus it is possible to distinguish among full adopters, partial adopters, interested persons or sympathizers, and indifferent persons. According to Elgin and Mitchell, 15 million consumers were full or partial voluntary simplifiers in 1977. In 1987, 60 million such simplifiers are predicted, and by the year 2000 there will be 120 million people subscribing to voluntary simplicity. Although these numbers may be upwardly biased, they certainly constitute a growing market segment that is measurable, accessible, and profitable. At the end of the 1970s this market segment was defined as young, well-educated, urban, of upper middle-class background, and almost exclusively white (Elgin and Mitchell 1977a; 1977b).

While the number of voluntary simplifiers was growing rapidly, the adherence of nonsimplifiers to economic growth and materialism was growing too, so that two distinct segments having extremely different philosophies of life seemed to be emerging (New York Times 1979).

Table 5.2 presents a comparison between voluntary simplifiers and those who are not simplifiers. As can be seen, the two groups are quite different in terms of values, and social and consumer characteristics. For example, while nonsimplifiers emphasize the value of material growth, and their social character therefore exhibits material complexity and specialized work roles, the simplifiers emphasize balance between material and spiritual growth, and their social character exhibits a preference for material simplicity and more integrated work roles. Such differences in the value systems and social characteristics of the two groups have an important impact on their attitudes and behavior as consumers. Nonsimplifiers value quantity, style, and impersonal outlets, whereas voluntary simplifiers emphasize quality, functionalism, and durability.

TABLE 5.2

Voluntary Simplifiers and Nonsimplifiers

Value Premises

Material growth	material sufficiency coupled with psychospiritual growth
People over nature	people within nature
Competitive self-interest	enlightened self-interest
Rugged individualism	cooperative individualism
Rationalism	rationalism and intuition

Social Characteristics

Large, complex living and working environments	smaller, less complex living and working environments
Growth of material complexity	reduction of material complexity
Space-age technology	appropriate technology
Identity defined by patterns of consumption	identity found through inner and interpersonal discovery
Centralization of regulation and control at nation/state level	greater local self-determination coupled with emerging global institutions
Specialized work roles through division of labor	more integrated work roles (such as team assembly, multiple roles)
Secular	balance of secular and spiritual
Mass-produced, quickly obsolete, standardized products	hand-crafted, durable, unique products
"Lifeboat" ethic in foreign relations	"Spaceship Earth" ethic
Cultural homogeneity, partial acceptance of diversity	cultural heterogeneity, eager acceptance of diversity
High-pressure, rat-race existence	"laid-back," relaxed existence

Consumer Behavior

Big is better	small is better
Preference for quantity	preference for quality
Preference for style	preference for the functional
Less emphasis on durability	more emphasis on durability
Ecologically and environmentally less responsible	ecologically and environmentally more responsible
Preference for big outlets (stores)	preference for small, personal outlets (stores)
Little receptivity to innovative outlets	more receptivity to innovative outlets, such as flea markets, street vendors
Less do-it-yourself orientation	more do-it-hourself orientation
Less co-op buying	more co-op buying
Television orientation	print and radio orientation

Source: Adapted from Elgin and Mitchell 1977a, p. 15.

117

The post-stagflation consumer is characterized not only by a new set of values but also by new expectations about the health of the economy and his or her ability to adjust to economic changes such as inflation. Consequently, the emerging post-stagflation consumer is one who considers the rate of inflation, both present and expected, as an important variable in purchase decisions. The result, of course, is new rules of thumb:

Conduct business transactions "off the books." This practice is becoming increasingly popular among consumers, workers, and businesses, who avoid paying taxes by using cash in their transactions. Peter M. Gutmann (1977) defined this part of the economy as "subterranean economy," and estimated that in 1976, $28.7 billions were used in the United States to generate about 10 percent of the American Gross National Product extralegally

Advance purchase, because money loses its value in comparison to other assets such as a house. Indeed, an increasing number of consumers, particularly young families, are driven by inflation to buy more (Hollie 1979), while others have postponed having children

Investing in real estate or buying a house, so that taxes are paid as real estate taxes rather than income taxes while the value of real estate appreciates

Saving less and spending wages before they are earned. For example, savings as a percentage of income have been significantly declining in the past four years (Kibborn 1979)

Using more credit because of low real interest and because interest payments constitute tax deductions. For example, while consumer installment credit outstanding in 1973 was about $125 billion, it became $275 billion by February 1979. Installment debt delinquencies have also increased (Wall Street Journal 1979).

It should be mentioned here that such rules of thumb are not unique to the American consumer. Many countries experiencing a high rate of inflation, such as Great Britain, Italy, France, Israel, and Chile, have operated under them. To a certain extent such countries may indicate what awaits the American society should inflation persist.

Consumer behavior in the post-stagflation era constitutes such a pronounced departure from behavior in the pre-stagflation era that some economists argue that a new "Econo sapiens" is emerging. The new economic man observes price movement and government economic policies, and reacts to them rationally—buying in advance, taking a higher mortgage, and so on. Combined, his reactions tend to reinforce inflation and to neutralize economic policies.

To marketing management, the immediate implications of changes in consumer motives, values, and expectations are marketing-mix adjustments relating to decisions concerning pricing policies, products, promotion, and distribution, as outlined in Table 5.1. Because of the increased importance that consumers attach to price, many have changed their shopping behavior, use of credit, and finances, which may require that marketing management price more strategically, adjust distribution and credit policy, and take advantage of the growing consumer need for financial management. In terms of products, because consumers have changed their attitudes toward product attributes, modifications in products and product-line pricing that result in relatively lower prices and functionalism may be desirable. In terms of promotion, because of changes in what consumers value, promotional appeal may be modified to stress lower prices and desired product attributes. Finally, distribution policy may be more receptive to simplification. The discussion and detailed report of the findings in Chapter 2 suggest clearly that marketing management is adapting to the changing consumer and his or her environment. In addition, a study examining stability and change in marketing methods reports that, compared with the 1960s, the 1970s were characterized by greater pricing efforts, smaller sales efforts, increased marketing research efforts, increased style and research and development efforts, and increased importance of branding and packaging (see Harris et al. 1978). These findings support the recommendations for marketing management made in Chapter 2.

The Post-Stagflation Employee

Stagflation has accelerated a process of decline in Americans' attitudes toward work so that the evolving work ethic increasingly views employment as an instrument for achieving economic gains. And when such an instrument does not enable satisfactory achievement of material growth, attitudes toward work become more negative, moonlighting rises, and more spouses and children join the labor force. Such changes represent new opportunities to marketers (for instance, how to keep the labor force happy and productive, thus keeping cost down).

It should be noted that federal policies often indirectly reinforce negative attitudes toward employment. For example, wage increases due to inflation often push employees into higher tax brackets, and federal wage guidelines, requiring that a company's average wage increases not exceed 7 percent annually, motivate employees to move from one company to another in order to obtain higher salary increases (the guidelines do not cover new employees).

The Post-Stagflation Family

Participation by family members in the labor force has increased because of stagflation. There have also been changes in the family role structure and in risk taking. Because money is tight, families have become more careful with money, and have shied away from purchase decisions involving high risk, and have made more decisions jointly. These changes require that marketing management change product design to appeal to husband and wife jointly, and that it use more risk-reducing promotional appeals. Two-wage-earner families represent new opportunities for marketers.

The Post-Stagflation Voter

Best symbolized by Proposition 13, the post-stagflation voter is clearly a new political species. He or she is more independent, confident, and daring, and believes in his or her ability to change things. This of course creates a totally new political climate for candidates and policy makers (see Chapter 3).

Marketing management should monitor changes in voter attitudes and behavior because such changes often imply changes in consumer behavior.

The Post-Stagflation Individual

The changes in people's attitudes and behavior as consumers, employees, family members, and voters represent basic changes in the individual's attitudes and behavior toward the social system to which he or she belongs, including its economic and political facets. Thus, the emerging post-stagflation individual is more skeptical about society's abilities to solve its problems, pessimistic about economic affairs, and aware of basic changes in his or her attitudes and behavior. Such changes trigger changes in consumer behavior that marketing management should monitor.

ECONOMIC POLICY DURING STAGFLATION

Traditionally, government economic policy has included monetary measures, fiscal measures, or both. Regardless of the type or combinations of measures, however, they have always been used in either expansionary or contracting policies—never simultaneously in both. However, it has been demonstrated in this book that stagflation represents a mixed economic environment that may call for expansionary measures and contracting measures simultaneously. Although this may sound contradictory, it nevertheless depicts economic realities during stagflation. As has been demonstrated, some industries may be experiencing a recession while others experience strong inflationary pressures. In such a situation the only effective policy measures are those that include stimulative measures targeted at depressed industries and contracting measures targeted at inflation-stricken industries. Thus, stagflation may require a mix of policy measures that traditional or Keynesian economic theory perceives as an impossibility.

Yet, in its role as a consumer, employer, regulator, and economic policy maker the federal government is capable of dealing with stagflation effectively. As the largest consumer in the country, the government may increase, decrease, or leave unchanged its demand for products and services from the various sectors and regions, depending on the nature of the impact of stagflation on such sectors and regions. As a regulator, the government may ease its requirements for those industries hardest hit by escalating costs, so that their cost of complying with federal regulations and the need to raise retail prices are minimized. Easing the emission-control regulations is a classic example. As the largest employer in the country, the federal government may have an impact on both the employment level and wage levels. This impact should be used as part of the national economic policy and not—as often is the case—as an unrelated matter.

Most important, however, is the government use of fiscal and monetary measures to implement economic policy. Yet, because stagflation requires different expansionary and contracting mixes simultaneously, basic moral values guiding economic policies must be reexamined. For example, if different industries are subjected to different policies, the equity of the policy is changed drastically—that is, moving from input equity (same policy to all industries) to output equity (similar policy results in all segments of the economy). Connected with this important issue are equally basic ones. For example, the output equity orientation requires more careful monitoring of the economy and large-scale interventions in economic matters. This, however, may negate basic beliefs concerning free enterprise and entrepreneurship. Nevertheless, it seems clear that federal economic policies, beginning with the various proposals for tax-based income policies and ending with the guidelines of the Council on Price and Wage Controls requiring a voluntary ceiling of 5.75 percent on annual average price increases by business and a ceiling of 7 percent on average wage increases, are clear signs of increased government intervention in economic matters.

122 / MARKETING IN A SLOW-GROWTH ECONOMY

Such interventions are expected to grow in the future, and marketing management should follow them carefully before making strategic marketing decisions.

MARKETING IN THE POST-STAGFLATION ERA

Changes within the social system in which marketing management operates have a direct impact on marketing strategy and marketing-mix decisions. Accordingly, the emerging post-stagflation consumer represents both new opportunities for marketing and new risks. To minimize risk and capitalize on opportunities, careful monitoring of consumers by means of consumer and marketing research is imperative. Similarly, careful examination of federal economic policies may reveal new possibilities and help minimize the impact of regulations.

But the above are short-run adjustments by marketing management. There is a growing consensus that for the long run, strategic planning is perhaps the most important activity in the post-stagflation era (see, for example, Hempel and La Placa 1975; Steiner 1979).

Strategic planning is the process of developing explicit courses of future business conduct designed to produce a desired growth rate and return on investment by "achieving market position so advantageous that competitors can retaliate only over an extended period of time at a prohibitive cost" (Kollat, Blackwell, and Robinson 1972, p. 12). Such a market position can be achieved by careful, broad-based, flexible, and future-oriented business plans and general courses of action—that is, strategies. Thus, strategic planning differs from the usual corporate planning in its longer-range orientation and its holistic approach. It is designed to know and understand changes in external, uncontrollable variables so that anticipated changes can be used beneficially. It facilitates more than "forearming by forewarning," in that it "seeks to optimize the 'fit' between a corporation and its future environment" (Wilson et al. 1978).

The characteristics of strategic planning are as follows (see, for example, Wilson et al. 1978; Koontz 1976; Hempel and La Placa 1975; Steiner 1979):

1. Holistic, systems approach. Marketing operates in a complex social, economic, and political system in which elements are interrelated. Unless marketing management has a broad view of its situation, it will operate in a myopically conceived environment, which may lead to strategic errors. This is particularly

true during periods of rapid environmental changes, as was the case in the second half of the 1970s and the expectations for the 1980s. Drastic changes in the environment include changes in economic realities, consumer behavior, societal values, and government policies. Though such changes cannot be controlled by marketing management, they can and should be monitored and used as inputs in the strategic planning process. For example, it is expected that the voluntary simplicity movement will grow rapidly and influence more consumers. Similarly, it is expected that economic growth will slow down, as will the demand of government for products and services. Such changes, which may not be directly related to a company's business, may nevertheless have a direct impact on its business in the future and should, therefore, be considered in the course of strategic marketing planning.

2. Long-run or future orientation. Strategic planning differs from the traditional corporate planning in its longer-range orientation—usually 5-20 years, and in its being less restricted to a given set of products or business decisions. In fact, because the anticipated seldom occurs, while the least expected often happens, there is a recognition that future orientation means that one should consider several possible futures. Therefore, strategic planning starts by outlining various scenarios depicting possible futures. Each such scenario contains predictions or assumptions about the social and political environments, as well as about economic and business conditions, that form an integrated depiction of a possible future. On the basis of the scenarios, strategic planners proceed to make one overall plan for each scenario, so that whatever scenario materializes in the future, there will be a clear plan of action.

For example, strategic marketing planners may prepare the following two scenarios for the 1980s: material growth will continue to be dominant, with its related values of "more is better" and material comfort; material growth will be less dominant, while the number of people returning to basics and simplifying their consumption pattern voluntarily will grow. On the basis of two rather opposite pictures of the future, contingency plans may be made so that management is prepared to respond to either future with specific business and marketing plans.

To avoid mistakes, an exhaustive list of scenarios of the future must be developed. Otherwise, the company may be confronted with unanticipated realities.

3. Flexible or "nothing is final" orientation. Strategic planning by definition tries to predict or establish possible futures, based on which profitable and satisfying business plans can be made. The

basic rationale for developing different pictures of the future is that the future may take different shapes, anticipated as well as unanticipated. Because of this, strategic planning must be flexible enough to allow the incorporation of additional possible futures, new variables, changes in the environment: strategic plans in which everything is final are myopic or too restricting.

4. Active or initiating orientation. Strategic planning does not try to respond only to possible future events. Rather, by trying to depict such futures, it may invent them to its own advantage. Thus, "The central dynamic of strategic planning is the conviction that . . . the forewarned corporation can help influence the course of events and reshape, on its own initiatives, its strategies, policies, and even its mission" (Wilson et al. 1978, p. 67). For example, in the post-stagflation era it may well be that marketing management helps to shape or accelerates changes in social values, economic growth, and government economic policies.

5. Goal orientation. Strategic planning's main goal is to improve a company's long-run performance on whatever criteria it selects: profits, growth, market share, or other. It is implemented because changes in the uncontrollable variables pose a threat to survival and to the achievement of long-run goals. Although strategic planning does not guarantee success, it increases its likelihood.

Although the main focus of this book has been the impact of stagflation on society and marketing management, stagflation has been conceived and treated as a major economic, social, and political issue. As such, it is shaping a future drastically different from the past and the present. However, the exact shape of the future social order depends on the degree of stagflation and on coping strategies used by people as consumers, voters, and individuals, and by marketing management and government policies. This will undoubtedly be the focus of much future research.

REFERENCES

Elgin, D., and A. Mitchell. 1977a. "Voluntary Simplicity (3)." CoEvolution Quarterly (Summer): 4-19.

_____. 1977b. "Voluntary Simplicity: Life Style of the Future?" Futurist (August): 200-16.

Gregg, R. 1936. "Voluntary Simplicity (1)." Reprinted in CoEvolution Quarterly (Summer 1977): 20-27.

Gutmann, P. 1977. "The Subterranean Economy." Financial Analysts Journal (November-December).

Harris, C. E., R. R. Still, and M. Cresk. 1978. "Stability or Change in Marketing Methods?" Business Horizons 21, no. 5 (October).

Hempel, J., and P. La Placa. 1975. "Strategic Planning in a Period of Transition." Industrial Marketing Management 4: 305-14.

Hollie, P. 1979. "Inflation Driving Young Families to Purchase More and Save Less." New York Times, April 23, pp. A1, D6.

Kibborn, P. 1979. "Consumer, Resigned to Inflation, Is Learning New Ways to Hedge." New York Times, April 22, pp. A1, A60.

Kollat, D., Blackwell, and J. Robinson. 1972. Strategic Marketing. New York: Holt, Rinehart, and Winston.

Koontz, H. 1976. "Making Strategic Planning Work." Business Horizons (April): 37-47.

Lazer, W. 1979. "The 1980's and Beyond: A Perspective." HSU Business Topics 27 (Spring): 21-35.

New York Times. 1979. "Study Finds Rise in Materialism amid Economic Gloom." May 9, p. C8.

Paul, N. R., et al. 1978. "The Reality Gap in Strategic Planning." Harvard Business Review 56 (May-June): 124-30.

Schoeffler, S., et al. 1974. "Impact of Strategic Planning on Profit Performance." Harvard Business Review 52 (March-April): 137-45.

Schumacher, E. F. 1974. Small's Beautiful: Economics as if People Mattered. New York: Harper and Row.

Steiner, G. 1979. Strategic Planning. New York: Free Press.

Wall Street Journal. 1979. "Consumer Debt Load, After Reaching Peak, May Signal Recession." May 8, pp. 1, 19.

Wilson, H. I., et al. 1978. "Strategic Planning for Marketers." Business Horizons 21 (December): 65-73.

GLOSSARY

BUDGET CONSTRAINT LINE. A theoretical conception of a "line" representing all combinations of products and services on which the consumer may spend income

CHANNELS OF DISTRIBUTION. The set of marketing intermediaries chosen by the producer in the effort to best fulfill the firm's objectives

CONSUMER PRICE INDEX. An instrument designed to measure the changes in the purchasing power of the consumer's dollar over time. It records the changes in prices of products and services (about 400) said to be consumed by a "typical" family of two adults and two children. It is the most popular measure of inflation, and the basis for labor negotiations and government policies.
  Effective with the January 1978 index, the Bureau of Labor Statistics began publishing CPIs for two population groups: 1. a new CPI for all urban consumers (CPI = U) which covers approximately 80 percent of the total noninstitutional civilian population; and 2. a revised CPI for urban wage earners and clerical workers (CPI = W) which represents about half the population covered by the CPI = U.

COST-PUSH INFLATION. A situation of rising costs of raw materials and production channels, characterized by production over-capacity and varying degrees of unemployment

DEMAND ELASTICITY. The sensitivity of purchasers to changes in price. When a price reduction increases sales and total revenue, demand is said to be elastic (elasticity greater than 1); when a price reduction decreases revenue, demand is inelastic (elasticity smaller than 1); and when price reduction increases sales but does not influence total revenue, demand elasticity is 1

DEMAND-PULL INFLATION. Characterized by full employment and too much money competing for too few goods and services

DISPOSABLE INCOME. Disposable personal income is derived by deducting the part that is taken by government in personal taxes from the total income from all sources of persons or households. It is the amount available for people to dispose of as they choose

126

ECONOMIC GROWTH. The increase in the economy's output; measured quarterly, semiannually, and annually

FIFO. An accounting method (first in, first out) in which the cost of the last items received are assigned to the ending inventory and the remaining costs are assigned to goods sold

FISCAL POLICY. The exercise of the government's control over public spending and tax collections to achieve the objectives of a given economic policy

GROSS NATIONAL PRODUCT. The total dollar value of all goods and services produced by an economy during one year

GROWTH RECESSION. An economy characterized by high rates of inflation and low rates of growth—in essence, a euphemism for stagnation

INFLATION. A persistent and appreciable rise in the general level of prices; a process of rising prices of raw materials and final products and services

INNOVATION. An idea, practice, or object perceived as new by an individual

LIFO. An accounting method (last in, first out) in which the costs of the last goods received are matched with revenue from sales

MACROECONOMICS. The study of relations between broad economic aggregates; the theory of income, employment, prices, and money; the part of economics that studies the overall averages and aggregates of the system

MARGINAL COST. The increase in the total cost of production associated with producing one more unit of product

MARKET SEGMENTATION. The process of isolating smaller, more homogeneous segments within a market, for the purpose of selecting one or more target markets and developing a unique marketing mix to satisfy the needs of each

MARKET SHARE. The percent of total sales that a given product or product line commands in a given market

MARKETING MIX. The decisions regarding product, price, place, and promotion. These are the controllable variables that a company combines in order to satisfy its target group and achieve a differential advantage over its competition

MICROECONOMICS. A field of economic inquiry in which the unit of study is the part rather than the whole. It is concerned with the output of particular goods and services by single firms or industries, and with the spending on particular goods and services by single households or by households in single markets

MONETARY POLICY. The exercise of the central bank's control over the money supply as an instrument for achieving the objectives of a given economic policy

MONOPOLY. A situation in which one seller dominates an industry by setting a higher price than would have been established by free competition

OPEC CARTEL. A cartel is an association of producers or suppliers to establish a monopoly, usually by price fixing. The Organization of Petroleum Exporting Countries established its cartel in the early 1970s to fix the price of oil in the international markets. Prices are always set at a level higher than would have been determined by free competition

OLIGOPOLY. A market situation that occurs when a few control a given market. Oligopoly develops when a market has essentially homogeneous products; relatively few sellers, or a few large firms and perhaps many smaller ones that follow the lead of the larger ones; fairly inelastic industry demand

PHILLIPS CURVE. A curve illustrating the inverse relationship between the rate of inflation and the rate of unemployment

PRODUCT LINE. A group of products that are closely related because they satisfy a class of needs, are used together, are sold to the same customer groups, are marketed through the same types of outlets, or fall within a given price range

PRODUCT MIX. The composite of products offered for sale by a firm or a business unit

PRODUCT PRUNING. A systematic set of activities designed to reduce the number of products in a given product line and thus to weed out those products not performing satisfactorily along a number of preselected criteria, such as profitability, market share, growth

PROMOTION. A communication process including advertising, personal selling, sales promotion, and publicity that business may use to influence its consumers and facilitate an increase in sales

PROMOTION MIX. The combined effort of advertising, personal selling, publicity, and sales promotion that a business may choose to increase the likelihood of achieving its goals

RECESSION. A situation of decreasing demand for raw materials, products, and services, including labor. In the United States a recession is said to exist when the GNP declines during two consecutive quarters

REPOSITIONING. The process of actively trying to improve the place a given product occupies in the consumer's mind relative to competing products. This effort includes changing the main concept or idea that the product represents, as well as other marketing-mix variables necessary to carry out the repositioning efforts

SHORTAGE. An economic and psychological state that occurs when demand is larger than supply at the existing price level

STAGFLATION. Any combination of inflation, recession, and shortages. There are four types: inflation-shortage; inflation-recession; recession-shortage; inflation-recession-shortage

STRATEGIC PLANNING. Developing plans for future activities that will increase the likelihood of achieving a company's goal; it is very long-range, and requires flexibility and contingency planning

SUPPLY ELASTICITY. The sensitivity of supply to changes in price. When a drastic change in supply is triggered by a small change in price, supply is said to be elastic; when even a big change in price does not trigger much change in the quantities offered in the market, supply is said to be inelastic

TARGET MARKET (OR TARGET GROUP). A fairly homogeneous group of customers that is the focus of marketing efforts

UNEMPLOYMENT. A rate representing the unemployed as a percentage of the labor force.

APPENDIX A:
ACCOUNTING FOR VARIANCE

Although variables that account for the differences in the impact of stagflation on consumers were discussed in Chapter 4, full multivariate knowledge was not provided. To achieve such knowledge, a stepwise regression was run for each survey, conceiving the general impact of stagflation (strongly positive to strongly negative) as dependent upon demographic, economic, employment-related, societal, and political variables (altogether, 59 independent variables).

Stepwise regression was chosen because it not only shows how much of the variance is explained by the independent variables, but also rank-orders the independent variables by relative contribution to explanation of the variance. The results of these analyses are presented in Tables A.1 and A.2.

As can be seen in Table A.1, the independent variables account for 53 percent of the variance in the impact of stagflation in 1976. The most important of these variables relate to education, consumer frustration, personal happiness, changes in family role structure, shopping behavior, purchase expectations, and income.

The minus sign next to a figure under "Beta" in Table A.1 represents a negative relationship between the impact of stagflation (range from strongly positive to strongly negative on a seven-point scale) and the independent variables (range from strongly agree to strongly disagree on a seven-point scale). Accordingly, the stronger the respondents' agreement about being frustrated as a consumer, the more negative the impact of stagflation.

It is noteworthy that important variables such as employment, age, and occupation rank among the last variables in explaining the variance. Race did not even enter the equation because the F level was too low. It is also noteworthy that education, consumer variables, and family role structure rank at the top.

Table A.2 shows that the independent variables explain almost 59 percent of the variance among the 1978 respondents. Ranking at the top were employment, car economy, medical care, personal happiness, and spouse's employment. Accordingly, more negative impact of stagflation was associated with the respondents' unemployment, high evaluation of economy in cars, putting off medical/dental care, spending more time shopping, unemployed spouse, and higher education. Again, socioeconomic variables such as race, occupation, and age rank rather low in explaining the variance.

TABLE A.1

Stagflation 1976: Explaining the Variance

Variable Rank	Variable Description	Multiple R	Beta
1	Education	0.181	0.097
2	As a consumer I am more frustrated than I used to be	0.266	-0.188
3	There are fewer new products on the market	0.304	0.131
4	Weigh purchase decisions with spouse more than I used to	0.325	-0.199
5	Become a do-it-yourself person	0.351	-0.127
6	Stop giving donations or give smaller ones	0.367	0.131
7	Look for cheaper products (such as private labels)	0.384	-0.087
8	As a consumer I have changed my habits and preferences	0.398	0.133
9	Must buy less of everything	0.413	-0.203
10	Employer: private or public	0.424	0.092
11	Energy-conscious	0.435	-0.147
12	Have to work harder to be able to afford present way of life	0.447	0.122
13	Put off car repairs	0.454	-0.070
14	I am less happy than I used to be	0.462	0.060
15	Income	0.470	0.095
16	More careful with money	0.474	-0.128
17	Less wasteful	0.481	0.176
18	More of a comparison shopper	0.487	-0.091
19	Argue about financial matters	0.491	-0.084
20	There are more low-quality products on the market than there used to be	0.496	-0.068
21	Political affiliation	0.499	-0.093
22	Cut down on luxuries	0.502	0.091
23	Spouse's employment status	0.505	-0.069
24	Spend less on hobbies	0.507	0.058
25	Judge products and services in a new way	0.510	-0.065

Variable Rank	Variable Description	Multiple R	Beta
26	Become insecure about my job	0.511	-0.036
27	Lose faith in the economy	0.514	0.080
28	Spend more time (on the average) shopping	0.515	0.059
29	Shop for "specials" and bargains	0.518	-0.064
30	Pay higher prices for products and services	0.520	-0.032
31	Visit family and friends more often	0.521	-0.060
32	Drive less	0.523	0.040
33	Spend more time reading	0.524	-0.055
34	Sex	0.525	-0.055
35	Spend more time at home	0.527	0.072
36	Use more credit	0.527	0.051
37	Pay bills late	0.528	-0.035
38	The variety of products is decreasing	0.529	0.050
39	Employment	0.530	-0.031
40	Put off medical/dental checkups or treatments	0.530	-0.038
41	Realize I can't really improve my economic position	0.531	0.038
42	Lose faith in government	0.532	-0.045
43	Repair durable goods rather than replace them	0.532	-0.034
44	Occupation	0.533	0.025
45	Harder to make financial plans	0.533	0.042
46	Age	0.534	-0.027
47	Save less	0.534	-0.025
48	Dine out less	0.534	-0.024
49	Minimize the use of utilities	0.534	0.013
50	Prices will be a lot higher in the future	0.534	-0.010
51	Look for more durability when shopping for durable goods	0.535	0.011
52	Marital status	0.535	-0.008
53	Must delay purchases of durable goods	0.535	-0.011
54-59	F level too low		

Source: Compiled by the author.

TABLE A.2

Stagflation 1978: Explaining the Variance

Variable Rank	Variable Description	Multiple R	Beta
1	Value fuel economy in cars	0.237	-0.132
2	Employment	0.308	-0.193
3	Put off medical/dental checkups or treatments	0.358	-0.245
4	I am less happy than I used to be	0.383	-0.074
5	Spend more time (on the average) shopping	0.402	0.061
6	It is harder to make ends meet	0.420	-0.152
7	Employer: private or public	0.450	0.123
8	Spouse employed	0.461	0.118
9	Pay higher prices for products and services	0.471	0.283
10	Save less	0.480	-0.086
11	There are fewer new products on the market	0.491	0.106
12	Education	0.499	0.098
13	Look for more durability when shopping for durable goods	0.507	-0.135
14	Spend more time reading	0.512	0.096
15	Spend more time at home	0.519	-0.082
16	Shop for "specials" and bargains	0.525	-0.115
17	Budget myself	0.533	0.135
18	As a consumer I have changed my habits and preferences	0.539	-0.139
19	Become a do-it-yourself person	0.543	0.039
20	Cut down on luxuries	0.547	0.098
21	Lose faith in government	0.550	-0.085
22	Prices will be a lot higher in the future	0.554	-0.104
23	It is harder to make financial plans	0.557	0.039
24	Spend more time watching television	0.559	-0.040
25	Look for cheaper products (such as private labels)	0.561	-0.053
26	More of a comparison shopper	0.563	-0.059
27	As a consumer I am more frustrated than I used to be	0.565	0.070
28	Income	0.568	0.118
29	Stop giving donations or give smaller ones	0.569	-0.068

Variable Rank	Variable Description	Multiple R	Beta
30	More careful with money	0.571	0.061
31	Buy more products through whole-sale outlets (such as clothing, appliances)	0.573	0.090
32	Race	0.574	0.051
33	Less wasteful	0.576	-0.059
34	Realize I can't really improve my economic position	0.577	0.033
35	Drive less	0.578	-0.068
36	Must delay purchases of durable goods	0.579	-0.048
37	Spend less on hobbies	0.581	0.052
38	Pay bills late	0.582	0.042
39	Minimize the use of utilities	0.582	0.053
40	Weigh purchase decisions with spouse more than I used to	0.583	-0.058
41	Occupation	0.584	-0.057
42	Marital status	0.585	-0.035
43	Repair durable goods rather than replace them	0.585	0.043
44	Must buy less of everything	0.586	-0.048
45	Dine out less	0.586	-0.005
46	Energy-conscious	0.587	-0.047
47	Use more credit	0.587	-0.040
48	There are more low-quality products on the market than there used to be	0.587	0.031
49	Variety of products is decreasing	0.588	0.028
50	Visit family and friends more often	0.588	-0.034
51	Become insecure about job	0.589	0.031
52	Political affiliation	0.589	0.019
53	I have to work harder to be able to afford my present way of life	0.589	0.013
54	Judge products and services in a new way	0.589	0.011
55	Sex	0.589	0.011
56	Age	0.589	0.011
57	Lose faith in the economy	0.589	0.009
58	Argue about financial matters	0.589	0.008
59	Do not take chances with new products any more	0.589	0.008

Source: Compiled by the author.

ACCOUNTING FOR THE VARIANCE SIMPLIFIED

It is possible to account for differences among consumers by using the factors from Tables 4.8 and 4.9 as new variables in the regression equation. This not only simplifies the process, but also takes care of the problem of multicollinearity, which is possible when data are not factor-analyzed. Again, the results (not reported) show that the most important variables in accounting for the variance among consumers relate to education, shopping behavior, purchase expectations, and income.

IMPACT AND ADJUSTMENTS: LINEAR OR CURVILINEAR RELATIONSHIPS?

A close look at the findings in Tables 4.4 and 4.5 leaves one puzzled as to why such a high proportion of consumers used the "strongly agree" and "agree" response categories on a seven-point scale. For example, of the sample of 969 consumers in 1976, the proportion agreeing or strongly agreeing was the following:

70.3 percent that because of stagflation it is harder to make ends meet
48.3 percent that because of stagflation they are frustrated as consumers
67.8 percent that because of stagflation they do more comparison shopping
57.7 percent that because of stagflation they shop for "specials" and bargains more than they used to
60.1 percent that in response to stagflation they look for wholesale outlets more than before.

Since both the 1976 and 1978 samples were large and heterogeneous (N_{1976} = 969 and N_{1978} = 916), it is logical to assume that the data represent the manner in which stagflation affects consumers, rather than biases associated with the samples per se. At work, one suspects, are second-, third-, and possibly fourth-order correlations between stagflation and resulting consumer adjustments. Such correlations postulate that the relationship between the general "impact of stagflation" variable (strongly positive to strongly negative; that is, the dependent variable) and specific changes in consumer behavior associated with it (such as expectations concerning future prices, shopping behavior, use of credit, life-style; that is, the independent variable) is curvilinear, such that second-, third-, and fourth-order correlations represent curvilinearity in progressing order. On the other hand, first-order correlation represents the usual linear relationship, shown in Figure A.1.

FIGURE A.1

Curvilinear (Polynomial) Regression: Possible Explanations of the Impact of Stagflation on Consumer Adjustments

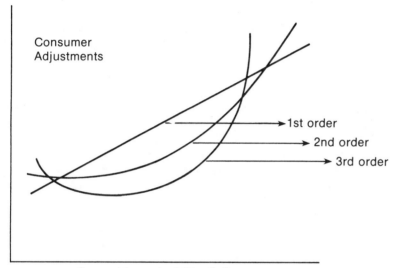

General Impact of Stagflation

Source: Constructed by the author.

In this context curvilinear relationships indicate that as the overall impact of stagflation becomes extreme (positive or negative), the resulting adjustments by consumers in terms of changing attitudes, life-style, and shopping behavior become even stronger. For example, respondents reporting a "somewhat negative" impact of stagflation would more than "somewhat agree" (that is, "agree" or "strongly agree") that as consumers they have changed their attitudes, life-style, and shopping and consumption behavior. If this is statistically supported, then it may be concluded that stagflation brings about changes in consumer behavior such that the dependent variable is related in a nonlinear manner (such as quadratic, cubic, or quartic) to the independent variable.

Since most researchers in this field seem to assume the linear relationship depicted in Figure A.1 (a first-order correlation), support for curvilinear relationships contributes to knowledge by its ability to correspond to reality more accurately. More specifically, if the proposition concerning curvilinear relationships is accepted, then the following are true:

1. Knowledge concerning how consumers cope with stagflation is gained, representing a contribution not only to marketing but also to economics and other social sciences.
2. Opportunities for marketing management represented by consumer groups extremely affected by stagflation (groups that are substantial, accessible, and profitable) arise as new markets or market segments can be more clearly delineated
3. Because stagflation represents the number-one economic, social, and political issue, its effect on consumers reaches far beyond marketing. Thus, the above contribution may represent a contribution by marketing to other disciplines.

To test for such suspected curvilinear relationships, the ith order correlation allowed by the stepwise multiple-regression computer program of the Statistical Package for the Social Sciences (SPSS) was used.* The dependent variable included 48 variables[†] representing possible changes in consumer attitudes, life-style, and shopping and consumption behavior due to stagflation.

Since the dependent variable (the overall impact of stagflation) included seven response categories, regression equations assuming sixth-, fifth-, fourth- (and so on) order correlations were recommended as common procedure and were run when testing for curvilinear relationships. The reasons for this are that it is impossible to determine curvilinearity a priori and that one should test all possibilities for such relationships.

The results of testing for the existence of first- (the usual linear), second-, and third-order correlations are presented in Tables A.3, A.4, and A.5, respectively. As can be seen in these

---

*When $i = 1$, the regression equation is a first-degree linear regression; when $i = 2$, the equation is a second-degree curvilinear regression (that is, it assumes a quadratic correlation between the dependent and independent variables), and so forth. (for pictorial presentation see Figure A.1.)

[†]Tables 4.4 and 4.5 include a partial list of dependent variables. The remaining dependent variables are similar.

tables, multiple R value for the 1976 data increases from 44.26 percent to 47.43 percent to 51.50 percent as one changes the assumption from first- (linear), to second- (quadratic), to third- (cubic) order correlations between the dependent and independent variables.* This represents a significant increase of over 7 percent in the ability to explain the variance among respondents with the same set of variables. This increment in the proportion of variance accounted for was tested with an F ratio and found significant at $P \leq .001$. The formula used was

$$F = \frac{(R_C^2 - R_L^2) \ / \ (K_C - K_L)}{(1 - R_C^2) \ / \ (N - K_C - 1)}$$

where

R_C^2 and R_L^2 are the proportions of variance accounted for, assuming cubic and linear relationships, respectively

K_C and K_L are the number of degrees of freedom, assuming cubic and linear relationships, respectively

N is the number of respondents.

Assuming fourth-, fifth-, and sixth-order correlations produced a decrease in the proportion of the explained variance in comparison with the assumption of third-order correlation.

Almost identical results (not reported) were obtained for the 1978 data. Consequently, it may be concluded that the relationships between stagflation and consumer adjustments are best represented by third-order (cubic) correlation. This means that as the effect of stagflation becomes extreme, the resulting changes in consumer opinion, life-style, shopping, and consumption behavior become much more extreme; in fact, cubicly so.

For the purposes of illustration, an examination of the first ten variables appearing in Tables A.3-A.5 may further enhance understanding of how stagflation affects consumers. These variables explain 38.9 percent, 42.2 percent, and 47.6 percent of the variance

---

*All variables listed in Tables A.3-A.5 produced significant F levels at $P \leq 0.05$ with n_1 and n_2 df. It should also be noted that as one changes the assumption from linear to quadratic to cubic (and so forth) relationships, one loses an additional degree of freedom at each step.

TABLE A.3

Stagflation and Consumer Adjustments: Stepwise Linear Regression, Assuming First-Degree Equation (linear correlation)

Because of stagflation (the independent variable) consumers adjusted by changing the following attitudes and behaviors (the dependent variable):	Multiple R	Beta
1 It is harder to make ends meet	0.22550	-0.16331
2 Put off medical/dental checkups or treatments	0.27091	-0.16179
3 Product variety is decreasing	0.30575	-0.09283
4 Shop for "specials" and bargains	0.32142	-0.09116
5 Spend more time (on the average) shopping	0.34109	-0.12412
6 Buy more products through wholesale outlets	0.35080	-0.06164
7 Realize I can't really improve my economic position	0.36106	-0.09351
8 Value fuel economy in cars	0.36970	-0.08691
9 Become a do-it-yourself person	0.37938	-0.12275
10 Become insecure about job	0.38943	-0.10453
11 Must delay purchases of durable goods	0.39666	-0.07635
12 Dine out less	0.40181	-0.09182
13 Spend less on hobbies	0.40573	0.06121
14 Drive less	0.40886	0.05873
15 Use more credit	0.41284	-0.05645
16 There are fewer new products in the market	0.41589	0.06095
17 More of a comparison shopper	0.41807	0.06584
18 Look for cheaper products (such as private brands)	0.42041	-0.02932
19 Repair durable goods rather than replace them	0.42262	-0.04994
20 I have to work harder to be able to afford my present way of life	0.42443	-0.06390
21 Cut down on luxuries	0.42691	-0.06256
22 Spend more time reading	0.42862	-0.05869
23 Save less	0.43004	-0.06212

Because of stagflation (the independent variable) consumers adjusted by changing the following attitudes and behaviors (the dependent variable):	Multiple R	Beta
24 Weigh purchase decisions with spouse more than before	0.43105	−0.04479
25 As a consumer I have changed my habits and preferences	0.43212	−0.03381
26 As a consumer I am more frustrated than I used to be	0.43299	−0.03304
27 Spend more time watching television	0.43381	−0.05097
28 Budget myself	0.43474	−0.03604
29 Put off car repairs	0.43554	0.03660
30 Pay higher prices	0.43642	0.03444
31 Prices will be a lot higher in the future	0.43709	0.03208
32 Judge products and services in a new way	0.43775	0.03200
33 Become energy-conscious	0.43845	0.03305
34 Stop giving donations or give smaller ones	0.43909	−0.02873
35 There are more low-quality products in the market	0.43965	0.02624
36 Lose faith in the economy	0.44014	0.02522
37 Visit family and friends more than before	0.44062	−0.03746
38 Become more careful with money	0.44121	0.03135
39 Spend more time at home	0.44159	0.02359
40 I am less happy than I used to be	0.44189	−0.02401
41 It is harder to make financial plans	0.44215	−0.01790
42 Do not take chances with new products	0.44240	−0.01985
43 Look for more durability in durable goods	0.44255	0.01285
44 Argue about financial matters more than before	0.44261	−0.00887
45 Less wasteful	0.44265	−0.00867

Note: All 45 variables (of the total 48) produced significant F levels at $P \leq .05$ with n_1 and n_2 df (N = 969). The results obtained from the 1978 study (not reported) are almost identical.

Source: Compiled by the author.

TABLE A.4

Stagflation and Consumer Adjustments: Stepwise Curvilinear
Regression, Assuming Second-Degree Equation
(quadratic correlation)

Because of stagflation (the independent variable) consumers adjusted by changing the following attitudes and behaviors (the dependent variable):	Multiple R	Beta
1 It is harder to make ends meet	0.26870	-0.19511
2 Put off medical/dental checkups or treatments	0.31026	-0.16173
3 Dine out less	0.33517	-0.10468
4 Spend more time (on the average) shopping	0.35290	-0.08372
5 Become a comparison shopper	0.36921	0.13230
6 Product variety is decreasing	0.38340	-0.11267
7 Realize I can't really improve my economic position	0.39555	-0.13548
8 Become insecure about job	0.40509	-0.12048
9 Buy more products through wholesale outlets	0.41680	-0.07947
10 Must delay purchases of durable goods	0.42199	-0.08063
11 Value fuel economy in cars	0.42912	-0.07644
12 Become a do-it-yourself person	0.43282	-0.11015
13 Prices will be a lot higher in the future	0.43830	0.06971
14 Look for cheaper products (such as private brands)	0.44163	-0.05225
15 Drive less	0.44509	0.04832
16 Save less	0.44747	-0.06914
17 Repair durable goods rather than replace them	0.44979	-0.05577
18 I have to work harder to be able to afford my present way of life	0.45178	-0.05501
19 Shop for "specials" and bargains	0.45401	-0.04925
20 Spend more time watching television	0.45587	-0.05019
21 Spend more time reading	0.45779	-0.05457
22 There are fewer new products in the market	0.45958	0.05581

Because of stagflation (the independent variable) consumers adjusted by changing the following attitudes and behaviors (the dependent variable):		Multiple R	Beta
23	Visit family and friends more than before	0.46099	-0.05106
24	Spend less on hobbies	0.46223	0.03181
25	Cut down on luxuries	0.46353	-0.04986
26	Use more credit	0.46500	-0.03805
27	As a consumer I have changed my habits and preferences	0.46630	-0.05590
28	Budget myself	0.46860	0.04231
29	Weigh purchase decisions with spouse more than before	0.46882	0.03683
30	As a consumer I am more frustrated than I used to be	0.46957	0.04009
31	Do not take chances with new products	0.47068	-0.03552
32	Put off car repairs	0.47115	0.02357
33	Spend more time at home	0.47171	-0.02892
34	Pay higher prices	0.47213	0.02613
35	Look for more durability in durable goods	0.47256	0.02732
36	Become energy-conscious	0.47302	0.02790
37	There are more low-quality products in the market	0.47336	0.01735
38	Lose faith in the economy	0.47364	0.02077
39	Lose faith in government	0.47385	-0.02032
40	Stop giving donations or give smaller ones	0.47409	-0.01568
41	Become more careful with money	0.47419	0.01335
42	Buy less of everything	0.47426	-0.00899
43	Less wasteful	0.47431	-0.01060
44	Argue about financial matters more than before	0.47435	-0.00704

Note: All 44 variables (of the total 48) produced significant F levels at $P \leq 0.05$ with n_1 and n_2 df (N = 969). The results obtained from the 1978 study (not reported) are almost identical.

Source: Compiled by the author.

TABLE A.5

Stagflation and Consumer Adjustments: Stepwise Curvilinear
Regression, Assuming Third-Degree Equation
(cubic correlation)

	Because of stagflation (the independent variable) consumers adjusted by changing the following attitudes and behaviors (the dependent variable):	Multiple R	Beta
1	It is harder to make ends meet	0.32463	−0.20294
2	Dine out less	0.36368	−0.13568
3	Put off medical/dental checkups or treatments	0.38589	−0.13177
4	Spend more time (on the average) shopping	0.40501	−0.16034
5	Become a comparison shopper	0.42043	−0.06820
6	Product variety is decreasing	0.43397	−0.09712
7	Realize I can't really improve my economic position	0.44816	−0.13455
8	Become insecure about job	0.46193	−0.10743
9	Must delay purchases of durable goods	0.47075	−0.08152
10	Buy more products through wholesale outlets	0.47646	−0.08699
11	Spend more time watching television	0.48017	−0.10671
12	Value fuel economy in cars	0.48384	−0.10203
13	Spend more time reading	0.48686	−0.06931
14	Visit family and friends more than before	0.48982	−0.06168
15	Shop for "specials" and bargains	0.49247	−0.07117
16	I have to work harder to be able to afford present way of life	0.49519	−0.06599
17	Become a do-it-yourself person	0.49765	−0.05271
18	There are fewer new products in the market	0.49984	0.06101
19	Look for cheaper products (such as private brands)	0.50167	−0.04830
20	Save less	0.50320	−0.03651
21	Drive less	0.50479	0.06028
22	I am less happy than I used to be	0.50589	−0.02076
23	As a consumer I have changed my habits and preferences	0.50674	−0.03213

Because of stagflation (the independent variable) consumers adjusted by changing the following attitudes and behaviors (the dependent variable):	Multiple R	Beta
24 Repair durable goods rather than replace them	0.50768	-0.04334
25 As a consumer I am more frustrated than I used to be	0.50844	0.02718
26 Put off car repairs	0.40930	0.03614
27 Do not take chances with new products	0.51002	-0.02555
28 Use more credit	0.51057	-0.02406
29 Look for more durability in durable goods	0.51106	0.03550
30 Spend less on hobbies	0.51147	0.02404
31 Lose faith in government	0.51182	-0.03635
32 Cut down on luxuries	0.51229	-0.02817
33 Judge products and services in a new way	0.51268	-0.02907
34 Prices will be a lot higher in the future	0.51298	-0.02436
35 Become more careful with money	0.51325	-0.02352
36 Lose faith in the economy	0.51361	0.02639
37 Buy less of everything	0.51394	-0.02509
38 It is harder to make financial plans	0.51419	-0.02727
39 Stop giving donations or give smaller ones	0.51438	-0.01650
40 Become energy-conscious	0.51450	0.01374
41 Spend more time at home	0.51464	-0.01508
42 Argue about financial matters more than before	0.51475	-0.01309
43 Weigh purchase decisions with spouse more than before	0.51486	-0.01530
44 Budget myself	0.51495	0.01340
45 Less wasteful	0.51504	-0.01456

Note: All 45 variables (of the total 48) produced significant F levels at $P \leq 0.05$ with n_1 and n_2 df (N = 969). The results obtained from the 1978 study (not reported) are almost identical.

Source: Compiled by the author.

among respondents with the respective assumptions of first-, second-, and third-order correlation. That is, the more drastic the impact of stagflation becomes, the more parsimoniously one can explain the differences among consumers in terms of consumer attitudes, opinions, and shopping activities, when one assumes third-order correlation (see Table A.5).

Note also that as a result of assuming nonlinear relationships, the rank order of the variables in Tables A.3–A.5 changes, sometimes significantly. For example, while "dining out less" was ranked twelfth with the assumption of linear correlation, it ranked second when assuming third-order correlation.

APPENDIX B:
QUESTIONNAIRE USED TO MEASURE
THE IMPACT OF, AND ADJUSTMENT TO,
STAGFLATION BY "FORTUNE 500" COMPANIES

Part I

Following are some questions about how inflation, recession, and shortage may have influenced your company. Please respond to each question by circling the number that best represents your answer.

Overall, to What Extent Has the Recent Period of Inflation, Recession, and Shortage Influenced:	A Great Deal	Considerably	Somewhat	Little	Not at All
1. Your company	1	2	3	4	5
2. Consumer credit	1	2	3	4	5
3. Consumer services	1	2	3	4	5
4. Selection of customers	1	2	3	4	5
5. Pricing policy	1	2	3	4	5
6. Product line	1	2	3	4	5
7. Product elimination	1	2	3	4	5
8. Promotion budget	1	2	3	4	5
9. Selection of promotion media	1	2	3	4	5
10. Promotion appeal	1	2	3	4	5
11. Sales force	1	2	3	4	5
12. Public relations	1	2	3	4	5
13. Research and development department	1	2	3	4	5
14. Channels of distribution	1	2	3	4	5

Part II

Following is a list of measures that you may have have taken in response to the impact of inflation, recession, and shortage that many companies have been experiencing in recent years. Please circle the number that best represents the degree to which you have taken each of the listed measures. If you have always practiced any of the listed measures, regardless of the present economic conditions, indicate so by circling the "not applicable" response category (6).

To What Extent Did Your Company Engage in Each of the Following Measures Because of the Recent Economic Stagnation:	Very Much	Much	Little	Very Little	Not at All	Not Applicable
15. Shifting the emphasis from sales volume to profit margin	1	2	3	4	5	6
16. Adding extra services and features to justify higher prices	1	2	3	4	5	6
17. Meeting the consumer's demand even if it means carrying items with marginal profits	1	2	3	4	5	6
18. Introducing substitute products for scarce goods	1	2	3	4	5	6
19. Developing alternative raw materials	1	2	3	4	5	6
20. Increasing research to improve long-range strategies	1	2	3	4	5	6
21. Increasing research to develop substitute products and innovations	1	2	3	4	5	6
22. Broadening the responsibility and role of the sales force	1	2	3	4	5	6
23. Increasing sales volume	1	2	3	4	5	6
24. Reducing sales force	1	2	3	4	5	6
25. Increasing sales force	1	2	3	4	5	6

26. Avoiding marginal accounts	1	2	3	4	5	6
27. Reexamining the distribution channels	1	2	3	4	5	6
28. Maintaining competitive prices rather than maximizing profits	1	2	3	4	5	6
29. Implementing stricter credit policies	1	2	3	4	5	6
30. Better servicing of faithful accounts	1	2	3	4	5	6
31. Reducing the product line to the more profitable items	1	2	3	4	5	6
32. Increasing use of discounts for slow-moving products	1	2	3	4	5	6
33. Reducing operating hours	1	2	3	4	5	6
34. Increasing investment in research for new raw materials	1	2	3	4	5	6
35. Increasing investment in research for substitute products and innovations	1	2	3	4	5	6
36. Capitalizing on new markets created by shortages	1	2	3	4	5	6
37. Reducing the promotion budget	1	2	3	4	5	6
38. Adjusting prices frequently	1	2	3	4	5	6
39. Increasing research in consumer behavior and expectation	1	2	3	4	5	6
40. Promoting the use of readily available products	1	2	3	4	5	6

41. Has your company taken any other steps to readjust its pricing, product, promotion, and distribution policies? If so, please list these steps below.

APPENDIX C:
QUESTIONNAIRE USED TO MEASURE
THE IMPACT OF, AND ADJUSTMENT TO,
STAGFLATION BY CONSUMERS

PART ONE

This part deals with the meaning of the present economic situation and its effects on you. Please answer each question or statement by circling the response category that reflects your opinion most accurately.

I. In general, the present economic situation has affected me 1. very much, 2. much, 3. somewhat, 4. not at all.

II. Would you say the effect was 1. strongly positive, 2. positive, 3. somewhat positive, 4. somewhat negative, 5. negative, 6. strongly negative.

III.

The Meaning of the Present Economic Situation Is That:	Strongly Agree	Agree	Somewhat Agree	Somewhat Disagree	Disagree	Strongly Disagree	Does Not Apply	Card 1 Col.
								(5)
								(6)
1. I pay higher prices for products and services	1	2	3	4	5	6	7	(7)
2. Prices will be a lot higher in the future	1	2	3	4	5	6	7	(8)
3. It is harder to make ends meet	1	2	3	4	5	6	7	(9)
4. I am more careful with money	1	2	3	4	5	6	7	(10)
5. It is harder to make financial plans	1	2	3	4	5	6	7	(11)
6. I am less happy than I used to be	1	2	3	4	5	6	7	(12)
7. I have to work harder to be able to afford my present way of life	1	2	3	4	5	6	7	(13)

	Strongly Agree	Agree	Somewhat Agree	Somewhat Disagree	Disagree	Strongly Disagree	Does Not Apply	Card 1 Col.
8. I must delay purchases of durable goods	1	2	3	4	5	6	7	(14)
9. I must buy less of everything	1	2	3	4	5	6	7	(15)
10. There are more low-quality products in the market than there used to be	1	2	3	4	5	6	7	(16)
11. As a consumer I have changed my habits and preferences	1	2	3	4	5	6	7	(17)
12. There are fewer new products in the market	1	2	3	4	5	6	7	(18)
13. I do not take chances with new products any more	1	2	3	4	5	6	7	(19)
14. People like me pay too much taxes	1	2	3	4	5	6	7	(20)
15. There is more advertising on television	1	2	3	4	5	6	7	(21)
16. There are more cents-off coupons	1	2	3	4	5	6	7	(22)
17. As a consumer I am more frustrated than I used to be	1	2	3	4	5	6	7	(23)
IV. The Recent Economic Crisis Has Made Me:								
18. More of a comparison shopper	1	2	3	4	5	6	7	(24)
19. Less wasteful	1	2	3	4	5	6	7	(25)

	1	2	3	4	5	6	7	
20. Cut down on luxuries	1	2	3	4	5	6	7	(26)
21. Shop for "specials" and bargains	1	2	3	4	5	6	7	(27)
22. Budget myself	1	2	3	4	5	6	7	(28)
23. Lose faith in the economy	1	2	3	4	5	6	7	(29)
24. Use more credit	1	2	3	4	5	6	7	(30)
25. Save less	1	2	3	4	5	6	7	(31)
26. Drive less	1	2	3	4	5	6	7	(32)
27. Spend more time at home	1	2	3	4	5	6	7	(33)
28. Become insecure about my job	1	2	3	4	5	6	7	(34)
29. Argue about financial matters	1	2	3	4	5	6	7	(35)
30. Look for cheaper products (such as private labels)	1	2	3	4	5	6	7	(36)
31. Dine out less	1	2	3	4	5	6	7	(37)
32. Visit family and friends more often	1	2	3	4	5	6	7	(38)
33. Buy more products through wholesale outlets	1	2	3	4	5	6	7	(39)
34. Stop giving donations or give smaller ones	1	2	3	4	5	6	7	(40)
35. Energy-conscious	1	2	3	4	5	6	7	(41)
36. Repair durable goods rather than replace them	1	2	3	4	5	6	7	(42)
37. Spend less on hobbies	1	2	3	4	5	6	7	(43)
38. Judge products and services in a new way	1	2	3	4	5	6	7	(44)

	Strongly Agree	Agree	Somewhat Agree	Somewhat Disagree	Disagree	Strongly Disagree	Does Not Apply	Card 1 Col.
39. Look for more durability when shopping for durable goods	1	2	3	4	5	6	7	(45)
40. Weigh purchase decisions with my spouse more than I used to	1	2	3	4	5	6	7	(46)
41. Spend more time (on the average) shopping	1	2	3	4	5	6	7	(47)
42. Pay my bills late	1	2	3	4	5	6	7	(48)
43. Put off car repairs	1	2	3	4	5	6	7	(49)
44. Put off medical/dental checkups or treatments	1	2	3	4	5	6	7	(50)
45. Minimize the use of utilities	1	2	3	4	5	6	7	(51)
46. Value fuel economy in cars	1	2	3	4	5	6	7	(52)
47. Become a do-it-yourself person	1	2	3	4	5	6	7	(53)
48. Spend more time watching television	1	2	3	4	5	6	7	(54)
49. Spend more time reading	1	2	3	4	5	6	7	(55)
50. Realize that I can't really improve my economic position	1	2	3	4	5	6	7	(56)
51. Lose faith in government	1	2	3	4	5	6	7	(57)

PART TWO

Now we would like to know the degree to which you spend more or less money on various products and services compared with last year. Please indicate how much more or less you spent in each product category by circling the appropriate number.

Compared with Last Year, How Much Do You Spend on Each of the Following:	A Lot More (30% or more)	More (about 20% more)	Somewhat More (about 10% more)	About the Same	Somewhat Less (10% less)	Less (about 20% less)	A Lot Less (about 30% less)	Card 1 Col.
52. Electricity	1	2	3	4	5	6	7	(58)
53. Gas	1	2	3	4	5	6	7	(59)
54. Telephone	1	2	3	4	5	6	7	(60)
55. Meat	1	2	3	4	5	6	7	(61)
56. Insurance	1	2	3	4	5	6	7	(62)
57. Canned foods	1	2	3	4	5	6	7	(63)
58. Frozen foods	1	2	3	4	5	6	7	(64)
59. Car upkeep	1	2	3	4	5	6	7	(65)
60. Children's clothing	1	2	3	4	5	6	7	(66)
61. Packaged foods	1	2	3	4	5	6	7	(67)
62. Adults' clothing	1	2	3	4	5	6	7	(68)
63. Hobbies	1	2	3	4	5	6	7	(69)
64. Entertainment at home	1	2	3	4	5	6	7	(70)
65. Gifts	1	2	3	4	5	6	7	(71)
66. Dining out	1	2	3	4	5	6	7	(72)
67. Cookies/candies	1	2	3	4	5	6	7	(73)
68. Movies/theater	1	2	3	4	5	6	7	(74)

	A Lot More (30% or more)	More (about 20% more)	Somewhat More (about 10% more)	About the Same	Somewhat Less (10% less)	Less (about 20% less)	A Lot Less (about 30% less)	Card 1 Col.
69. Magazines	1	2	3	4	5	6	7	(75)
70. Books	1	2	3	4	5	6	7	(76)
71. Newspapers	1	2	3	4	5	6	7	(77)
72. Travel	1	2	3	4	5	6	7	(78)
73. Soft drinks	1	2	3	4	5	6	7	(79)
74. Beer/liquor	1	2	3	4	5	6	7	(80)
								Card 2 Col.
75. Education	1	2	3	4	5	6	7	(7)
76. Car driving	1	2	3	4	5	6	7	(8)

PART THREE

Now we would like to know the extent to which, in your opinion, various factors are responsible for the economic crisis and how the crisis should be resolved.

To What Extent Do You Feel Each of the Following is Responsible for the Present Economic Situation?

	Very Responsible	Quite Responsible	Somewhat Responsible	Do Not Know	Somewhat Not Responsible	Quite Not Responsible	Not at All Responsible	Col.
77. President Ford	1	2	3	4	5	6	7	(9)
78. Congress	1	2	3	4	5	6	7	(10)
79. Arab oil embargo	1	2	3	4	5	6	7	(11)
80. Grain deal with Soviet Union	1	2	3	4	5	6	7	(12)

To What Extent Should Each of the Following Measures Be Included in the Solution of the Present Economic Problems?

	Should Definitely Be Included	Should Be Included	May Be Included	Do Not Know	Might Not Be Included	Should Not Be Included	Definitely Not Included	
81. Labor unions	1	2	3	4	5	6	7	(13)
82. Farmers	1	2	3	4	5	6	7	(14)
83. Big business	1	2	3	4	5	6	7	(15)
84. Mayor Beame	1	2	3	4	5	6	7	(16)
85. Governor Carey	1	2	3	4	5	6	7	(17)
86. Lowering prices	1	2	3	4	5	6	7	(18)
87. Increasing employment	1	2	3	4	5	6	7	(19)
88. Offering safer products	1	2	3	4	5	6	7	(20)
89. Offering more nutritious products	1	2	3	4	5	6	7	(21)
90. Offering product variety	1	2	3	4	5	6	7	(22)
91. Reducing advertising	1	2	3	4	5	6	7	(23)
92. More government regulations	1	2	3	4	5	6	7	(24)
93. Better service to consumers	1	2	3	4	5	6	7	(25)
94. More "cheap" private brands	1	2	3	4	5	6	7	(26)
95. Higher taxes	1	2	3	4	5	6	7	(27)
96. More government help to the poor	1	2	3	4	5	6	7	(28)
97. Higher prices for luxuries, lower prices for necessities	1	2	3	4	5	6	7	(29)
98. Consumer pressure on government	1	2	3	4	5	6	7	(30)

	Should Definitely Be Included	Should Be Included	May Be Included	Do Not Know	Might Not Be Included	Should Not Be Included	Definitely Not Included	Card 2 Col.
99. Lower taxes	1	2	3	4	5	6	7	(31)
100. Tightening one's belt	1	2	3	4	5	6	7	(32)
101. Making products more available at wholesale outlets and/or wholesale prices	1	2	3	4	5	6	7	(33)

PART FOUR

This part includes statements concerning opinions, interests, and activities. We would like to know the degree to which you agree or disagree with each statement. Please circle the response category that reflects your opinion most precisely.

	Strongly Agree	Agree	Somewhat Agree	I Don't Know	Somewhat Disagree	Disagree	Strongly Disagree	Card 2 Col.
102. When I go out shopping, I sometimes get the feeling that the merchants are just out to cheat me	1	2	3	4	5	6	7	(34)
103. Shopping is great fun	1	2	3	4	5	6	7	(35)
104. The worst part of shopping is the high prices	1	2	3	4	5	6	7	(36)
105. My choice of brands for many products is influenced by advertising	1	2	3	4	5	6	7	(37)

162

No.	Statement								Col.
106.	A store's own brand is usually just as good as a nationally advertised brand	1	2	3	4	5	6	7	(38)
107.	Shopping is serious business for me	1	2	3	4	5	6	7	(39)
108.	If I had more money, I would spend more on food	1	2	3	4	5	6	7	(40)
109.	I will probably have more money to spend next year than I have now	1	2	3	4	5	6	7	(41)
110.	Our family is too heavily in debt today	1	2	3	4	5	6	7	(42)
111.	No matter how fast our income goes up, we never seem to get ahead	1	2	3	4	5	6	7	(43)
112.	What America needs is more individual initiative	1	2	3	4	5	6	7	(44)
113.	Now is a good time to buy a car	1	2	3	4	5	6	7	(45)
114.	Now is a good time to buy a house	1	2	3	4	5	6	7	(46)
115.	Most big companies are just out for themselves	1	2	3	4	5	6	7	(47)
116.	Big companies are to blame for the way prices keep going up	1	2	3	4	5	6	7	(48)
117.	Government is to blame for the way prices keep going up	1	2	3	4	5	6	7	(49)
118.	The government should control prices and profits	1	2	3	4	5	6	7	(50)
119.	Generally speaking, I like to vote on election day	1	2	3	4	5	6	7	(51)
120.	People like me don't have any say about what the government does	1	2	3	4	5	6	7	(52)

		Strongly Agree	Agree	Somewhat Agree	I Don't Know	Somewhat Disagree	Disagree	Strongly Disagree	Card 2 Col.
121.	I consider myself a member of the silent majority	1	2	3	4	5	6	7	(53)
122.	By and large, I think politicians are doing a good job of solving our problems	1	2	3	4	5	6	7	(54)
123.	It makes me mad when I think about how much money people make on second-rate products	1	2	3	4	5	6	7	(55)
124.	Business spends too much lobbying and not enough improving consumer products	1	2	3	4	5	6	7	(56)
125.	Sometimes I feel that we are living on the edge of disaster	1	2	3	4	5	6	7	(57)
126.	My life is anxiety-ridden	1	2	3	4	5	6	7	(58)
127.	It is hard to get a good job these days	1	2	3	4	5	6	7	(59)
128.	In a job, security is more important than money	1	2	3	4	5	6	7	(60)
129.	I take pride in my job	1	2	3	4	5	6	7	(61)
130.	I get paid what I am worth	1	2	3	4	5	6	7	(62)
131.	I wish I had a different job	1	2	3	4	5	6	7	(63)
132.	I would like to have my boss's job	1	2	3	4	5	6	7	(64)
133.	Success in business is largely a matter of luck	1	2	3	4	5	6	7	(65)

134. There is too much advertising
on television   1   2   3   4   5   6   7   (66)

135. Television commercials really
make sense   1   2   3   4   5   6   7   (67)

136. Magazines are more interesting
than television   1   2   3   4   5   6   7   (68)

137. I usually consult Consumer
Reports or similar publications
before making a major purchase   1   2   3   4   5   6   7   (69)

138. Advertising sells a product, often
without telling the truth about it   1   2   3   4   5   6   7   (70)

PART FIVE

Please answer the following questions concerning your background.

139. Employment: 1) employed   2) unemployed   3) homemaker   4) retired   5) student   (71)
(If checked "1," go to question 140; otherwise go to 141.)

140. For whom do you work?   1) New York City   2) other public sector   3) have my own business   (72)
4) private industry

141. Occupation: Which of the following comes closest to your occupation? (If unemployed, check your last
occupation; if homemaker, check your husband's occupation; if student, check father's
occupation; if retired, check your last occupation.)

1) workman/laborer   2) operator   3) craftsman   4) service   5) clerical
6) sales   7) professional   8) managerial   9) other (please specify) _____   (73)

142. Income: What is your annual combined family income?

1) $4,999 or less   2) $5,000-9,999   3) $10,000-14,999   4) $15,000-19,999
5) $20,000-24,999   6) $25,000-29,999   7) $30,000-40,000   8) $40,000 or over

165

143. Marital status: 1) single 2) married 3) divorced 4) widowed 5) separated (If checked item 2, go to 144; otherwise go on to 145.) (75)

144. Is your spouse currently employed (or seeking employment)? 1) yes 2) no (76)

145. Age: 1) under 18 2) 18-24 3) 25-34 4) 35-49 5) 50-64 6) 65 or over (77)

146. Generally, I think of myself a(an); 1) Democrat 2) Republican 3) independent 4) other (please specify) _____ (78)

147. Sex: 1) male 2) female (79)

148. Race: 1) black 2) Caucasian 3) Oriental 4) Hispanic 5) other (please specify) _____ (80)

Card 3 Col.

149. Education: highest grade completed: 1) elementary school or less 2) some high school 3) high school 4) some college 5) college graduate 6) hold degree(s) beyond bachelor (7)

150. Residence: 1) Manhattan 2) Bronx 3) Queens 4) Brooklyn 5) Richmond 6) Long Island (Nassau, Suffolk) 7) New Jersey 8) Westchester 9) upstate New York 10) none of the above (please specify) _____ (8)

151. Interest in the results of this study: 1) yes (please write down your name and address.) 2) no (9)

152. Please write down any comments or thoughts that you might have concerning this questionnaire. Use other side of this page for your comments.

Thank You for Your Help.

166

ABOUT THE AUTHOR

AVRAHAM SHAMA is an Associate Professor of Marketing at Baruch College of the City University of New York. On leave from Baruch College, Dr. Shama is a Senior Policy Analyst at the Solar Energy Research Institute, Golden, Colorado.

Dr. Shama has published widely in the areas of consumer psychology, marketing management, and social change. His articles have appeared in the <u>Journal of Marketing</u>, <u>Journal of Advertising</u>, <u>Journal of the Academy of Marketing Science</u>, and the <u>Journal of the Society of Management Science and Applied Cybernetics</u>. His book on social change in Israel was published by Schenkman Publishing Company in 1977.

Dr. Shama holds a B.A. and an M.A. from the Hebrew University, Jerusalem, and a Ph.D. from Northwestern University in Evanston, Illinois.